TRANSFORMING FAMILY BUSINESSES

FROM DYSFUNCTIONAL TO EXTRAORDINARY

BY JIM KWAISER, CMC
WITH CONTRIBUTION BY ANN MARIE KWAISER

Transforming Family Businesses
From Dysfunctional to Extraordinary

© 2017 Jim Kwaiser, CMC
with Contribution by Ann Marie Kwaiser

NOTICE OF RIGHTS

Manufactured in the United States of America. No part of this book may be reproduced, transmitted in any form or by any means—electronic, or mechanical—including photocopying and recording, or by any information storage or retrieval system, except as may be expressly permitted in writing by the publisher or author.

NOTICE OF LIABILITY

The information in this book is distributed on an "as is" basis, for informational purposes only, without warranty. While every precaution has been taken in the production of this book, neither the copyright owner nor the publisher shall have any liability to any person or entity with respect to any liability, loss, or damage caused or alleged to be caused directly or indirectly by the information contained in this book.

ISBN-10: 1546725725

ISBN-13: 978-1546725725

CONTENTS

Introduction 1
Chapter 1   Just Get Along 7
Chapter 2   Communicate as Equals 15
Chapter 3   Have a Written Vision and Share It 23
Chapter 4   Address the Unspeakables 33
Chapter 5   Learn to Forgive 43
Chapter 6   Let Go of the Pecking Order 51
Chapter 7   Expand Your Advisors 63
Chapter 8   Never Dictate 75
Chapter 9   Get Your Priorities Straight 87
Chapter 10   Enlighten with Personal Experiences 99
Chapter 11   Set an Example 107
Chapter 12   Family and Feelings from a Woman's Perspective 119
Chapter 13   An Extraordinary Family in Business 127
Final Comments from Jim 137
Recommended Publications and References 141

ACKNOWLEDGEMENTS

There are a great number of people who have encouraged me over the years. First my partner in business and in life, Ann Marie who has always been at my side and helped me "transform' into the person I am today. To my daughters, Jennifer and Julieanne and their families who have brought me joy. To all our family businesses for allowing me to do God's work. To the Kwaiser and Geno families who put up with me bugging them for feedback.

A very special thanks to Jeff Tobe (www.jefftobe.com), whose encouragement set me on this writing path and who is a true friend (and to Judy too!). Thanks to Kathleen Dixon Donnelly (www.kdonnellycommunications.wordpress.com), our editor, who has become my first gypsy friend and certainly has helped me become a better writer. To Lisa Thomson (LisaT2@comcast.com) our formatter and designer who was very patient and offered suggestions well beyond her assigned task. To all of you – Thank you.

Contact Jim and Ann Marie Kwaiser
www.challengesinc.com
www.kabusinessplanners.com
jim@challengesinc.com
ann@challengesinc.com

INTRODUCTION

Life is full of challenges. When we decided to incorporate our company, and work exclusively with family businesses, we wanted a name that truly described what we do. "Challenges" was the name that immediately came to the minds of our daughters, Jennifer and Julie. We liked it but began to second guess it. Webster defines challenge as confrontation and, while that may be a fit for many families in business, we did not think that described exactly what we did.

We decided to do a little more research. While a contest, competition, dispute and confrontation are some of the definitions associated with challenges, and present in all family businesses, we found that the meaning went deeper. A test of ability and skill, taking on something new and different which requires change, effort and determination—all added together, brought us closer to the definition we were looking for. This deeper meaning included a conscious commitment to change, to try new things, even when they stretch an individual's abilities. We knew we had found our name.

We then decided to use the name as an acronym. First, to identify the steps of our process, and next to identify, for ourselves, how each would tie to our biblical principles. C.H.A.L.L.E.N.G.E.S., Inc. was born.

Our family business C.H.A.L.L.E.N.G.E.S. process is identified in the titles of chapters two through eleven. Each process offers lessons learned from working with families in business.

Lessons shared by true stories can be effective teachers for each member of a family business. The family business stories in this book cover a variety of C.H.A.L.L.E.N.G.E.S. while offering practical, objective solutions to the challenges each family business faces. Names and descriptions of the families and businesses identified in this book have been changed to maintain their privacy.

Transforming Family Businesses is an accumulation of stories, based on actual events of families who work together. Each story is a representation of a step in our C.H.A.L.L.E.N.G.E.S. process. We have written it for four major reasons.

The first is our passion, our mission, to help more families in business survive from generation to generation by implementing a process that has proven to be successful. A process and passion we believe is our charge in life to pass on to others. A process and passion that is guided by our practice of our Christian values and our responsibility to demonstrate those values to others, by our attitude, words and actions.

The second is our desire to teach families in business how to better understand the importance of dealing with the individual emotions of family members. Emotions that will have a major impact on relationships, longevity and the success of the family business.

The third reason is to introduce families in business into the FAMILY FIRST process and coach them how best to make use of it.

Our fourth reason is to help stop the erosion of family businesses. The Family Firm Institute and other publications have stated that two-thirds of family businesses do not make it past the second generation. This is unacceptable and we want to help lengthen the life of family businesses.

For families in business to survive a transformation must take place, changing the majority of families in business who believe that dysfunctional is normal. In the years I have been dealing with families in business I have yet to meet one that, in some way, doesn't view their family business as dysfunctional.

One family business we worked with described family businesses as "tricky." The relationships between working family members can be easily stretched, and even broken, because of unaddressed emotional issues. Tricky when the business is being run by family rules instead of business policies and procedures. Tricky when there is disrespect, dictatorships, conflict, overblown egos, and distrust. Tricky because many emotional

TRANSFORMING FAMILY BUSINESSES

and operational dysfunctions of the family are described as "normal" by most family businesses. The tricky and dysfunctional issues are addressed in each chapter of this book through the true stories described.

If family businesses are to lower the failure rate and beat the odds of being another statistic, they must transform from the dysfunctional to the extraordinary.

In working with families in business we have learned that the commitment of each family member to the success of one another—what we call FAMILY FIRST—reduces the risk of family business failure. Learning the process of how to discuss and commit to FAMILY FIRST within a family business, while implementing its principles, has proven to draw families closer together, and help businesses be more successful. The process and its principles are developed for you in the pages ahead.

Loving parents, even loving families, when dealing with the emotions brought out by working together can at some level always be called dysfunctional in the way their challenges are addressed and dealt with. Dysfunctional in the way they communicate and interact with one another. Dysfunctional when it comes to fairness, trust and loyalty. This book will show you how to transform from the dysfunctional to the extraordinary. Each chapter of this book includes a story that identifies

challenges a specific family in business is dealing with. Each story offers suggestions on the "how to's" that can help the family improve relationships and the business be more successful. Each chapter identifies what the family decided and the impact of their decision—or lack of one—on the family and the business.

When your family reviews each story, studies the decisions made, and learns how those decisions transformed the business, your family will become aware of new options to make your business more successful. In each chapter there are ideas for discussion (known as Kwaiserisms) that can be used to open up the communication and begin addressing your family's C.H.A.L.L.E.N.G.E.S.

With our combined experience of over 60 years in working with hundreds of families in business, we have observed what works and what does not. The following pages can help your family to understand the experiences of other families in business and how they dealt with their challenges. The experiences described in these stories will also help with your objectivity as they enable you to understand the options available, how the decision were made, and what the outcome was, good or bad. Each family decision is impacted by the emotions of the family, the changing market, the type of business and the make-up of the family members. Learning from others who have gone through these challenges is the best way to adapt to each situation for the benefit of your family and business.

Many of the families we work with pray together before meetings, major decisions and when planning direction. We agree with and encourage this practice as we understand and believe in the power of prayer. We have observed what prayer can do and experienced it as well. It certainly can't hurt!

We have also included a list of reference books, newsletters and websites used for material in this book.

We know that the information provided, along with the commitment of your family, can help you family identify the best, most practical way to transform your family business from dysfunctional to extraordinary. Thanks for choosing our book, and let us know how we can assist your family and your business.

www.challengesinc.com

JUST GET ALONG

*From dysfunctional to extraordinary
by putting FAMILY FIRST*

"Just get along" is what moms say to their kids. As a family business moves from one generation to the next we find that mom was right. To be successful, families in business together must find the right ways to "Just get along." Common sense and practical experience tells us that a business, especially a family business, would be more successful, more innovative and more productive if everyone in the family just got along better.

Unfortunately, for most family businesses the mindset is, "We are normal; we're dysfunctional."

> **THE JACKSONS**
>
> Steve and Debbie Jackson worked together in the family business with their two sons, Ted and Stuart, and a daughter, Kathy. The adult children did not get along, but they hadn't started out that way. In the beginning, all five came to work early, took their jobs seriously and stayed until the day's priorities were accomplished. They all had their individual jobs to do, and their full schedules most days left little time for one another. The tasks, the job, and the business became priority. They did meet once a week for a business update from Steve.

The rest of the time Debbie, Ted, Stuart and Kathy worked under the direct supervision of Steve.

The Dysfunctional

Steve felt that separation of his children, in responsibility and direction, would help them avoid the conflict that he felt had destroyed the relationships and companies of other family businesses he knew. Yet, as is usually the case, the more the family members in a business avoided one another the more suspicious of the intent of one another grows.

When sales and profits began to decline, the siblings started to blame one another. They did not know how decisions were made by the others, would only place blame on the other divisions and not their own, and argued for what they felt was right for themselves instead of what was the right decision for the company. They pulled further apart. Their families did not come together for functions other than weddings and funerals, and even then there was little interaction.

Debbie was devastated. She always wanted a family who loved one another, protected one another, and got along even with the extended family. She wanted to see all her children and grandchildren as one close, happy family. She was ready to have Steve sell the business as it seemed to get in the way of her desire to have her family "Just get along."

Stay tuned for the rest of the story.

When families make getting along better a priority by placing FAMILY FIRST, we have found that their businesses do better as well. This is because they will reach consensus on decisions faster with total family buy-in, while blending the family and the business. FAMILY FIRST adds to the understanding that the success of each family member is based on the success of everyone in the family. They then strive to assist each other in being the best they can be. You will read more about the importance of FAMILY FIRST throughout the upcoming chapters.

"Just getting along" is not as easy as it may sound. Families have curious ways of dealing with one another.

KWAISERISM

It is nice to be important, but it is more important to be nice!

When the children are young the parents repeatedly tell them how much they are loved and shower them with hugs and kisses. Even brothers and sisters may hug each other and often tell one another that they are "best friends." As each grows older, the times for sharing their love for one another become few and far between. They get used to other parts of their lives getting in the way of their family relationships. In a family business, poor communication can lead to lack of trust as well as strained and split relationships. Why do we let this happen? Let's switch gears for an explanation.

The Extraordinary

FAMILY FIRST is a conscious act by each member of the family to place the feelings, needs and success of other family members before their own. FAMILY FIRST should be the priority before each business decision is made. The decision-maker should consider how any decision may affect other family members, and if it will be in the best interest of the family and the business. If the decision does not benefit both, the family needs to be consulted first. FAMILY FIRST is when there is unconditional trust of the motives behind each family member's decisions, and the understanding that no decisions are being made for personal or selfish reasons.

If families are going to get along better, they need to get to know one another better. Do we really know what the others believe in? Have we

taken the time to find out? Spending quality time with one another, learning about the beliefs and values of each family member, helps us find common ground to "just get along."

All family members do not think alike nor believe in the same things. They do not always have the same points of view. When they don't acknowledge these differences, they won't get along. When they do acknowledge these differences as well as the right of each family member to have his or her own opinions, getting along becomes easier.

Out of love for your family, you know when to "bite your tongue and taste the blood," to move away from those areas that will keep you from getting along. Debate is okay, even arguing sometimes. But these are not okay when they rise to a level of emotional harassment that may severely strain or break the relationships.

This subject of "just getting along" caused me to think more about quality time with our families. We seem to make less time for the living and yet we will go out of our way to honor them when they are dead. I believe that "just getting along" must include spending more quality time with those we love.

We take time to remember those who have passed, but we need to remember how we got along with them when they were alive. The following story is offered for your consideration as an example of love, respect, honor and maybe even a little guilt for not being with a loved one when they were alive, just because the weather is bad or the timing is not right.

FROM JIM KWAISER

My mother passed away in Saginaw, Michigan in December, and on the day of the funeral the weather was rain and turning to snow. Yet people came from out of state, from Northern Michigan and other distances to pay their respects, even though the driving conditions were not the best. I began to ask myself, Why? Certainly, they loved my mom or were close enough to one of the remaining family members to come and pay their respects. But why now? Why at the funeral?

People will travel many miles for many hours to attend a funeral. But when it comes to visiting someone when they are alive, they have many excuses as to why they cannot take the time. Why do they wait? Wouldn't it be better to visit people when they are alive? Not only the deceased, but the other relatives that we have not seen or visited in years—or at least since the last family funeral!

THE JACKSONS, PART TWO

Debbie kept at Steve to do something to bring the family together. She saw her family splitting further apart and wanted that to stop. We were contacted to discover if we could help. We found jealously, distrust and an "I am out for myself" attitude among Ted, Stuart and Kathy. Stuart was the most extreme as he felt he should be running the company and have the highest compensation package.

We asked each of the family members to commit to weekly facilitated communication meetings. The objective was to have conversations about all challenges before major decisions are made, using consensus whenever possible, and to allow no surprises for any family member. They were to be informed before actions took place. They were not to openly speak critically about another family member or allow any employee to do so. We also had them schedule one on one meetings with one another, for better understanding of each other's wishes for the future and what they viewed as their role in it.

These techniques, along with facilitation of meetings and planning sessions, combined with a realistic view of how succession would impact each of them slowly, moved them toward mutual commitment and respect. They began to spend more time together as part of the process and found that they liked one another's company. The most difficult part pertained to the in-laws who lived with years of negativity about the family and now were asked to let all those feelings go.

Steve, Debbie, Ted, Stuart and Kathy are getting along better. The grandchildren have adapted to renewing their relationships with their cousins. The in-laws are not quite there yet, but the rest of the family is hopeful.

Other Thoughts

Just taking the time to ask yourself why relationships may be strained in your family and look realistically at what role you may being playing in that strain, can move relationships to a more positive position. Relationships take work and we all need to take the time to renew our relationships with friends and family. Don't take your family relationships for granted. You can transform dysfunctional family relationships into the extraordinary by family commitment, open communication and the very strong desire to "just get along."

CHAPTER 2

COMMUNICATE AS EQUALS

Nothing happens without effective communication

One of the most difficult aspects of effective family communication is addressing each member as an equal. Parents and children communicating as equals—what a concept! You might think that this could never happen. Communicating as equals is the most important and most difficult of the communication challenges in a family business. You may have observed or experienced parents who do unusual things to communicate with their children, such as twisting a child's ear to stress a point. This is not a practical way for equals to communicate; a child wouldn't communicate with the parent using that method! This is an example of communication between parent and child that is not equal.

This unequal communication often continues as the child grows into adulthood. The parents make the decisions and the father runs the business. Including the adult children in the decisions concerning estate or succession planning is not even considered. Why would you ask the opinion of the person whose ear you twisted? You were not equals then, how can you be now? Besides, mom and dad have always made decisions for the good of the children.

Childhood memories and perceptions of their meaning to relationships have a profound effect on communication in the family business environment. The communication of parents to children, children to parents, sibling to sibling, and even husband to wife are impacted by incidents experienced and perceptions formed from these memories. Perceptions become unspoken truths and will have a significant impact on whether family members will ever achieve communication as equals. The personal interpretation of these memories gives children the perception that their parents "just don't understand" or are "too old to know how I feel." The children feel as though mom and dad stick to the old ways of doing things and will never try anything new or different. As adults in a family business, the children tend to bring these feelings, this emotional stuff, with them into adulthood, hampering their ability to communicate with their parents as equals. Communication as equals between siblings and other relatives can even be harder to achieve.

THE MARKUSES

Cousins Joe and John Markus grew up in the family business that grandpa founded over 75 years ago; their fathers worked together running the business, got along well, and when it came time to pass it on, decided John was best suited for operations and Joe for the executive administrative side.

Joe, being the eldest, was named President and John was named Executive Vice President. Neither was asked what they thought. Neither was asked if they wanted an executive position with a great company. Their fathers knew that John and Joe never saw eye to eye on the direction of the company, but felt that they would get along in exchange for the rewards the business could provide. John felt they should grow the company any way they could and that he was the best to lead the organization. Joe believed that the company should stick with its core products and grow in a controlled, inter-industry fashion. He also believed that he could control John's actions. Neither had any real research or background information that supported their position. They both based their opinions on emotion, gut feeling and overinflated ego.

The Dysfunctional

Joe and John openly battled with one another in front of employees and vendors. They were different as day and night and saw the differences in one another as weaknesses and not strengths. They did not understand each other, never took the time to really get to know each other, and therefore did not care for each other. They saw themselves in competition for the leadership role and not as working together for mutual success. Not an unusual feeling in many family businesses.

One of the prominent emotional reasons most family businesses are considered dysfunctional/normal is the lack of demonstrated caring for one another, like the interaction of John and Joe. This includes the inability of family members to accept as strengths the behavioral differences of one another. When these differences are not appreciated the family places itself in the normal and dysfunctional category.

Joe and John really did not know one another on a personal level and their fathers never saw that as an important issue. Without that knowledge, you are going into business with a stranger whom you have been told to trust. Unless things change the business will not last.

Stay tuned for the rest of the story.

The Extraordinary

Communicating as equals in a family business must begin by preparing rules of communication within the family and the business. The family should start early, when the children are young, but few families do this with the business future in mind. Assigning duties in the business to each child, no matter how unimportant or how trivial the task may seem, makes each child feel that they are a part of something bigger. Because they have duties and responsibilities in the business, they have a sense of being equal to others.

KWAISERISM

If dysfunctional is normal for most families in business, causing business disruption and family strain, who wants to be normal?

Having each family member give a report on the progress of their assigned duties at a family business meeting creates a "communication as equals" sense of pride. Even the children can give a short presentation on their areas of responsibility. Assigning duties and requiring a report at meetings will foster responsibility and set a pattern that supports communicating as equals.

This approach requires commitment from everyone involved. A difficult commitment. This means treating all family members as equals for the expertise, knowledge, and skills they possess, as well as the tasks that they perform that contribute to the success of the business and the well-being of the family.

Communicating as equals applies to all family members, including spouses. Often in a family business, the spouse is left out of the communication loop, especially when he or she is not working in the business on a day-to-day basis. Business issues are not discussed because the spouse is seen as having nothing vital to contribute. Those working in the business sometimes forget that the problems, concerns, and situations of the company are brought home and can adversely affect a marriage. Never downplay the force of "pillow talk" in a family business.

Communicate with your spouse. Keep them involved by being open, honest, and clear in your description of business situations, especially when they involve relationships with other family members. Ask for their opinions. This will enable you to consider situations from a different point of view, which can be invaluable in making sound business decisions. This will also emphasize the "communicate as equals" approach throughout the family.

If this component is not consciously practiced in the family business, effective working relationships, strategic initiatives and consensus decisions will be almost impossible to achieve.

The extraordinary also appears when each participating member gives up competing with one another, when each family member makes a commitment to know one another as adults and not with preconceived notions from childhood. This happens only when everyone is committed to viewing the family and family business as a team, and begins to appreciate what each member can contribute to the success of each other. This can be tricky to accomplish and yet can produce above normal results.

Not everyone in the family business must always like one another, but they do have to trust and respect one another. Differences of opinion must give way to mutual success or the family and the business will suffer.

When unconditional caring and love are used as a guide to each family member's attitude toward one another, the family business will become extraordinary faster, and the legacy of the business will be more assured.

THE MARKUSES, PART TWO

The Markus family came to us for help, but neither Joe nor John would commit to make the necessary changes. We cannot help anyone who is not willing to place the success of

> the family before their individual success. Before long Joe and John's personal differences got in the way. They refused to really communicate with one another. They would not allow any room for compromise and both began to act independently of one another. By not working in conjunction with one another, they found themselves unofficially collaborating in destroying a great company. Sales and cash flow dropped. Good people left, and soon not much will remain of the company.

Other Thoughts on Open Communication

Most company leaders rarely consider communication as a process. Many have no formal process of how to communicate with family, managers and employees. Missing agendas, dictation instead of discussion, and the attitude of "We don't need to meet because we are talking every day" become the building blocks for communication failure.

When a process that includes:

- agendas,
- discussions on all topics,
- input on all decisions by key managers, as well as
- the manager's responsibility to drive communication throughout the company

The key is to have a process that is used consistently. When this happens who is in what role, or who is a long-time employee, or who is new, become less important. The successful process includes more than one individual and they all are aware of what is expected. Everything begins and ends with communication.

How communication is handled within a family determines whether there will be positive or negative actions between family members, and is eventually reflected in the results of the business. When families are young, confusing communication and emotions take place between siblings as they jockey for position in the family. Unfortunately this jockeying usually carries over to adulthood. Since most of these emotional issues between siblings, often including extended family members, were never resolved, they become unspoken stressors. Stressors that affect interpersonal relationships as well as family business decision-making. Poor communication can be viewed as a personal challenge or attack and is usually emotionally based. When there is no compromise, and little thought as to what is in the best interest of the family, everyone's goal becomes winning for themselves.

Someone wins and someone loses is a poor combination for any family and a disaster for a family business.

When poor communication is treated as a challenge to be conquered together, the results will be positive for the family. Communication will no longer be viewed as a win/lose proposition pitting one family member against another. Each issue is viewed as being important to the harmony and success of the family and addressed with the respect that each family member deserves. When each potential issue is given this type of respect, and the family finds solutions together, the result is stronger relationships, and because of those relationships, a more successful business.

Many families in business avoid addressing communication issues because they fear the conflict or potential conflict that will come to the surface. They just don't want to deal with the conflict in their hope for family harmony. Usually, the opposite takes place. These unspoken issues are like a virus in the minds of the family members. Everyone is affected and individual stress grows: Stress that will lead to conflict issues that will lead to confrontation that will lead to more stress, conflict and confrontation. A vicious cycle.

Too many families in business fail. Most fail due to destroyed relationships caused by the inability to communicate effectively. Key among these issues include how succession is handled and how well the family deal with personal and emotional issues. Without a good communication process, without the commitment to open communication, without the commitment to change and to care for one another, families in business will be truly dysfunctional.

CHAPTER 3

HAVE A **WRITTEN VISION** AND **SHARE IT**

Restructuring how families in business work together

This step involves defining, in writing, what the company means to the parents and explaining this to the children. The company must mean more than just financial opportunities. The dreams, hopes, and business ethics of the parents must be included. The children need to conduct the same exercise and share it with their parents.

Sharing the vision identifies what the parents would or would not do for the achievement of profits or increased business. The vision describes the business values of the parents, including understanding how customers, vendors, and employees should be treated. The parents and the children who will eventually take over must talk about and understand how the values and culture of the parents will be a central focus of the company for years to come.

Restating and sharing the vision between parents and children allows for better understanding of the mission, goals, and value positions of the parents, in language appropriate for each child's age level.

By starting to communicate the vision at an early age, the children can formulate a clear picture of the real meaning of the family business. Without this understanding, the children will have inaccurate perceptions of the family business, making up their own answers to those questions left unanswered by the parents.

Combining the mission, vision, and value convictions into one written philosophy statement—one short, meaningful description of what the company means and stands for to the parents—is helpful in insuring a consistent explanation to all the children as they grow into adulthood.

As they take a more active role in the business, how the children view the philosophy of the company should also be understood by all family members. In this way, parents and adult children are able to identify those areas where there is agreement and those areas that need additional explanation, before the transfer of the business takes place.

Amazing as it may seem, some parents cannot understand why their children may choose a different career, even though the parents have never communicated the positive sides of being involved in the family business. One heir apparent to a successful company was asked why he did not want to enter the family business. He explained that while he was growing up, all he could remember was his Dad complaining about the

employees, vendors, and customers, while his Mother was always upset because Dad was never home at a regular time to eat dinner. The heir apparent stated, "Why would I want to go into a business that made my parents so miserable?" He had made up his own response to Mom and Dad's perceived attitude toward the business, as he interpreted their words and actions.

Parents often are unaware their children are constantly watching and listening to them, and live out what they have heard or observed. Parents sometimes disregard the fact their children will make lasting judgments based on what they, as parents, say and do. These judgments and impressions remain with the children as they grow into adulthood. Identifying the philosophy of the business and discussing this with potential successors are vital parts of the communication process. There have been parent-founders who have spent years training and preparing their children as potential successors only to find out too late that the successor never agreed with the existing, underlying company philosophy. The result is the parents watch their dreams become their nightmare. The successors might begin to use business practices the parents do not condone, causing the philosophy foundation, upon which the company was built, to crack and decay. Communicating in writing the philosophy of the business and spending time to be sure the others are willing to accept it, live it, and carry it forward can save a lot of heartache and headaches for the parents and the adult children alike.

This has been found to be most often neglected when successors are considered and chosen. This neglect can be tragic, as the philosophy of the parents is usually the heart and soul of the business.

The Importance of Having Written Rules and Roles

Families and family businesses usually operate by two different sets of rules. In families, for the most part, parents are in control; they give the orders and everyone follows them. There is usually unconditional acceptance of the parents. Most decisions are made by them; the children are protected because their basic needs are met by someone else.

The business rules are different, or at least should be. The owners and managers are in control, everyone must pull their own weight and produce. All must make decisions regarding their tasks, and earning a living is the only way to meet basic needs. Rules should be a little different in the business compared to how it was when the children were small and living at home. In many cases, families still try to run the business as a family, based on the memories they had of how things were when the children were small.

THE FELLS

The Dysfunctional

Jerry and Marg Fells had four sons, Chris, Ken, Ron and Don, all involved in the family business. Each one was known for certain behaviors as children. Chris was known for losing his temper and getting loud; Ken for easily getting his feelings hurt; Ron for trying to be the mediator; and Don for avoidance of any conflict until he was backed into a corner.

The brothers remembered what each of their siblings had done well and where each had really screwed up. The Fells' sons, as many do, brought those memories into adulthood. They based their judgements and opinions of one another as adults upon their childhood memories. They interacted with one another based on those memories.

Stay tuned for the rest of the story.

"He has always been like that," are words we hear often in family businesses. The problem is rarely do the siblings take the time to know one another as adults. They haven't taken the time to find out what their siblings believe in, what they will or won't do to succeed, or how they view the future. They really don't know how their siblings feel about life, fairness and trust.

Unfortunately, many parents haven't taken the time either, so many of their opinions are also based on when the children were small and living at home. Treating a family business like a family with the same baggage from childhood is a major ingredient in the recipe for failure. Too bad so many "normal" families do exactly that!

The Extraordinary

In a family business, each family member and employee must be given a written job description with accountability and authority responsibilities. Each must know what they can and cannot do without authorization of the other family members. In a family setting you may only need mom and dad's approval; in a family business approval should be required from all working family members.

A lot of people disagree with us on this one, yet we have found many conflicts arise when working family members are shut out of decisions others make but also affect their areas of responsibility. How would you feel if another family member made decisions you should have been making? If that is how decisions are currently made in your family business then you are living "normally" and may truly understand dysfunctional as our definition of normal!

KWAISERISM

Family and family business cannot be separated.

Rules on how meetings should be conducted, a family code of conduct, a company and family mission statement, job descriptions, including the accountability and responsibility mentioned earlier, along with any other potential conflict issues, need to be developed and put in writing. These rules of conduct and communication should also include the founder's business values and ethics so there is not any confusion over what is expected from family members in running the business. Each person should be on a work schedule that is known, understood and committed to. People can't be coming and going without others involved in setting the schedule.

Most family businesses have rules about how to do certain tasks. The written rules we are describing here go further than just tasks; they need to include how the family and employees conduct themselves to the public and to each other. This should include family trust first and the FAMILY FIRST philosophy and rules.

Family and family business cannot be separated. The emotions and experiences move with each family member into the workplace. Identifying what rules stay and what new ones are needed is a must for the successful transition from family to family business.

THE FELLS, PART TWO

Jerry and Marg Fells had a working family members meeting. When asked why they acted the way they did, Chris stated the only way he could be heard when he was small was to yell and lose his temper. Ken said the more emotion he showed as a youngster, the more attention he got. Ron said he hated conflict and wanted to end it so he never took sides and tried to find the middle ground for everyone. Don stated he did not want to get in any fights, that he usually knew what needed to be done, but no one asked, so he just did it himself.

The more they talked the more they realized they had brought these behavior traits with them into the business. They also realized if they kept those old behaviors, they would miss a great opportunity to use the strengths of everyone, grow the business, and have the family be more successful for the future.

The Fells drew up new written policies in which none of the brothers could bring their old behaviors to a meeting. They even had a "kiddie" jar in which each brother would have to put in $5 every time he reverted to his own childish behavior.

This worked for them. There was greater respect for one another and their contributions, more sophisticated written rules about behavior, and much better operating results.

Do they ever slip? Yes. In fact, Chris was the biggest contributor to the kiddie jar during the first two months, but now ranks third.

> Ron has taken the lead in $5 donations as he still has a difficult time contributing to the conversation; he is beginning to realize this not only costs him money, but costs the family business his vital input. The Fells have begun the journey of moving from the "normal/dysfunctional" to "above normal." They are excited to be taking this trip together.

Written Roles Have to Be Objective

Many families in business make the mistake of placing someone in a position because they think it will be a great fit. When it doesn't turn out that way everyone is surprised. For the security of the family each position should be filled by the best qualified individual. Any family member who is not ready should be assessed to determine what areas they need to strengthen to do the best job, and then help them develop in those areas.

Objectivity is difficult in a family business when it comes to filling positions. We recommend having an outside family advisor assess family members for key positions. Putting the right person in the right spot is a major factor for a continued legacy in a successful business.

Other Thoughts on Written Rules and Roles

Written rules and roles are for everyone in the family business. No exceptions. Responsibilities, accountability and authority must be known and understood by every family member and employee.

Your employees cannot report to everyone in the family. Who reports to whom must be understood and honored by all in the company. The family working together in an open, honest way should develop, commit to, and support the written rules and roles.

Yes, mom and dad, you need to set the example by following the rules as well. This is one of the best ways you can coach and mentor your potential successors. When they observe you keeping the rules, they will follow your lead. Each role is different and all should understand the contribution that each makes to the success of the business. This brings a much better environment into the workplace and above normal, innovative thinking to each role. Not a bad place to end up.

Other Thoughts
The First Rule for Every Family in Business to Develop: Have a Written Code of Conduct

Loyalty and trust are two of the building blocks of successful family relationships and successful family businesses. They should be the centerpiece of your family and business code of conduct, which must be put into writing. Loyalty and trust should be automatically *given* and not forced upon one another. If each family member realizes, and commits to, love of the family includes loyalty and trust, then relationships will be enhanced and the company will grow and profit as it should.

Are You Trusted?

Are you trusted by your employees? While production and sales can grow with leaders who motivate by fear, trust produces sustained and positive morale, innovation, loyalty and results. Real trust must be earned and that does not happen overnight.

As the head of the company you earn trust through your attitude, words and actions in the following ways:

1. By your attitude, by your commitment toward your people, the company and the future as the number one cheerleader;
2. By your words, by communicating in a clear, concise and humble manner while you continually learn and teach;

3. By your actions, doing the right things, demonstrating compassion and character, while leading others to results that are beneficial to all.

Trust can also be fleeting. David Horsager, in *The Trust Edge* says, "Trust is like a forest. It takes a long time to grow yet can burn down with just one careless act." Be wise. Prepare yourself so your attitude, words and actions will be trusted and your careless acts will be few. When trust is present rules will be followed, roles will be taken seriously, and the family and employees will all work together. Be honest with yourself—Do you trust others? Do others trust *you*?

CHAPTER 4
ADDRESS THE UNSPEAKABLES

THE THREE SCHELL BROTHERS

As children, brothers Jerry, Jim, and Dick Schell decided to set up their own savings bank at home. The three brothers, not yet teenagers, contributed a portion of their income from their paper route and odd jobs to the bank on a weekly basis. Jerry, the eldest, was the self-designated banker.

The stash of saved money would be used for a future, mutually beneficial activity. In most cases, that activity would be centered around a treat of steak sandwiches, fries, and malts at the local Tony's restaurant. This activity became a monthly ritual that was always looked forward to with great anticipation.

On one of these days, Jim and Dick went to Jerry to collect their money for the anticipated feast. Jerry informed them the bank had gone bust because of a bad loan to himself. Jerry, the banker, had drained the bank and spent the money on himself and his friends, for a trip to Tony's!

The Dysfunctional

Now they are adults, do not ask Jim or Dick to vote for Jerry as the financial officer of the family business. They remember his cavalier attitude toward money, and they certainly do not want him in charge of a bigger bank account now. The fact Jerry was 12 at the time has little relevance. Jerry took money that was not his and spent it.

After graduating college, Jim and Dick went into their dad's hardware store business. They had helped there through high school and college and loved working with their dad. Jerry, who became a CPA, decided to go to join some larger accounting firms in hopes of working his way up to partner.

Within five years he became a partner in a firm, but was putting in more hours than he ever thought possible. The money was great but the effort was placing a strain on his wife and kids. He decided to talk to his dad and see if he could do the accounting for the family company.

The lone hardware store had now grown to five locations and a financial officer was warranted. His brothers now owned 50% of the business and Dad stated that they would have to be the ones to make the decisions. Jerry even offered to purchase 25% of Dad's stock so he could show his commitment to the family and business. Dad thought it was a great idea and did not see problem. He was confident Jim and Dick would be enthusiastic about their brother coming into the business. Dad had not heard about the money incident, so little did he know how wrong he was!

Stay tuned for the rest of the story.

Childhood experiences like this can establish a negative lifetime perception. The adult perception of a brother or sister is imprinted in our subconscious and stays with us into our adult lives. Issues such as the home bank incident, when left unaddressed, impair communication on an adult level. When this happens, trust and openness needed for the family business to thrive is next to impossible. Without honest communication, running a family business is all but hopeless.

Overcoming the mindset of the parent-to-child, and child-to-child dialogue is difficult to achieve. We have observed adults being treated like children by their parents, even when the children are over 50 years of age! In addition, there are times when adult children have difficulty relating to their parents as adults, as they revert to the role of a child, by enabling Mom and Dad to make all the major business decisions, just like when they made all the family decisions. A new mindset in family communication must be achieved when it comes to the operation of a family business. The children and parents will eventually become partners and one day the children may run the business. Treating your business partners with the usual mindset most parents and children use will not work.

Imagine a business where the decisions of the partners are considered either too childish by the parents, or too old fashioned and not up-to-date by the adult children, or too immature by the siblings. Family members who cling to the old ways of family communication doom the company to failure. These same family behaviors from childhood are handed down from generation to generation, adding to the difficulty of open communication and threatening the continuation of the family business. Conflict is born by lack of openly communicating about what we call the unspeakables.

"Unspeakables" are those feelings and perceptions which have been left unsaid by individual family members to avoid conflict, promote harmony, and avoid hurting the feelings of one another. The result of this behavior is just the opposite of what is intended.

The Extraordinary

A family owned business always carries the potential for uncertainty, vagueness, conflict and dysfunction. How the family members work together, communicate with one another, build on one another's strengths and care for one another will have a major influence on whether the family and business will evolve from normal/dysfunctional to the extraordinary. Letting "unspeakables" fester can easily destroy the trust family members have for one another.

Family businesses can become extraordinary but they must turn away from thinking of dysfunctional as normal. Open, honest, communication, even when difficult, will open the door to trust and enable the magic of extraordinary to be achieved by the family. Extraordinary results take place when the entire family subdues their personal ego for the success of the business and family. Having the courage to understand how we may have negatively affected another family member, to listen without becoming defensive, to realize that we may be the center of the "unspeakables"—this is a tipping point all members of the family must come to.

KWAISERISM

It is what is not said that kills relationships.

When the family has a shared belief that individual security is attainable only through the success of the family, by each family member looking out for and being sensitive to the needs and feelings of one another, will extraordinary be achievable.

Dealing with the unspeakables is like stirring a large pot of water, symbolizing open communication. This pot is where the unaddressed emotions, negative feelings, impressions, and perceptions believed by members of the family about other family members reside. These unspeakables are the sludge and debris that is hidden in the bottom of the pot.

Effectively addressing these unspeakables can only happen when the debris and sludge rise to the surface, as the communication pot is stirred. Every time you address these tough issues, you stir up that sludge and debris. Some of the stuff on the bottom floats up and clouds the liquid. This can make communication seem unclear or even worse than before the stirring.

But stirring the pot is necessary. Without stirring, hurt feelings, misconceptions, and misunderstandings cannot be addressed and skimmed off. This stirring and skimming for many families is usually avoided and is rarely achieved. This avoidance creates more "stuff" that goes into the pot. Stuff such as suspicion, for example, adds to the sludge and debris, building up in the pot to the point where the waters of open communication are quickly spilled out and, usually, gone forever.

Communicating as equals takes commitment and so does addressing these unspeakables. The family needs to commit to allow the emotional sludge and debris to be stirred up, and then to have the courage to address each issue as adults, as equals. Without communicating as equals, families and the business can easily be pulled in several directions, causing hurt feelings and an unsure future.

The unspeakables are carried with them into adulthood and, when left unaddressed, will interfere with the decisions, plans, direction, and success of the family business.

THE SCHELL BROTHERS, PART TWO

Dad met with Jim and Dick to discuss Jerry's proposal. While all three brothers got along well socially, went together to family functions, and even mixed well with each other's wives and kids, both Jim and Dick balked at the thought of working together. A CFO who steals! They did not want to be looking over their shoulders at their brother. Neither wanted a suspect financial officer.

Jerry's successful career meant little; nor did his offer to pay cash for 25% of the shares from their parents. They remembered the emotion they had felt as 10 and 11-year-olds. They told their dad "No." Jerry could not come on board. They contacted Jerry, had a very professional meeting with him and…

Stay tuned for the rest of the story.

When the unspeakable is carried into adulthood and left unaddressed, this issue will interfere with the decisions, plans, direction, and success of the family business.

The story of Jerry who took the bank of money as a child and is now passed over for chief financial officer of the family business is a good example of an unaddressed unspeakable.

Unspeakables could and have involved family members who feel they have been snubbed by an in-law. Instead of addressing this situation, the individual allows it to affect the relationship with their family members, usually with a sibling who is married to the troublesome in-law.

Unspeakables can build up until one day a small incident subconsciously reminds a person of the other hurts they have collected. People can lose their tempers and overreact to minor occurrences.

Sometimes this is based on unrealistic perceptions of a relative, who has had an honest career and a strong desire to be close to family. The real issue may have happened years before, but was left unspoken and unresolved. These issues influence each person's attitude toward one another. An attitude that focuses on the unfair way that they perceive they have been treated in the past can have negative effects on the family and the business.

Family members in a business must take the plunge into the communication pot and address those unspeakables. They have to address the tough issues. Conflict cannot be avoided forever. Nothing should be left unsaid concerning the personal issues that will eventually affect the ongoing success or failure of the business.

Virtually all festering personal issues left unaddressed will affect the business. In the majority of cases, when personal unspeakables are not addressed, trust is compromised, good judgment is second guessed, and immediate decisions are delayed—ironically, all in the name of family and business harmony.

Family rules do not usually prepare children to handle conflict as adults. Children are taught not to argue with their brothers and sisters, nor talk back to mom or dad. They are often disciplined for being honest. When a young person says, "Aunt Linda's coat is ugly" (and it really is!) mom and dad probably said, "If you don't have something nice to say, then don't say anything at all."

Most parents have taught their children to avoid conflict, especially if the message, even if true, could hurt someone's feelings. Avoiding conflict causes the unspeakables to grow inside of children. As they grow up, behaviors of their siblings or parents that have bothered them for a long time, maybe years, have never been openly discussed. Decisions that mom, dad, brother, or sister may have made for them when they were younger can be viewed by the affected person as wrong or unfair, and remain an unspeakable for many years. These feelings of unfairness will affect trust, as in the example of brother Jerry, and can hamper effective business-decision making—for example, when purchases are stalled due to the feeling that a parent or sibling may not want to spend any money.

Bitter battles among family members have occurred, not necessarily because someone might be wrong or that their decision will be bad for the family or the business, but merely because of one person who feels "I am an adult now and you can no longer tell me what to do." In these battles, most of these feelings can be directly traced back to an unspeakable. Some action, word, or misconception which occurred in the past still causes hurt feelings and fosters the perception of family members being unable to extend trust to another.

An effective way to uncover the unspeakables is during an "Address the Unspeakables" session. These sessions should be conducted by an independent facilitator.

Each family member is asked to write a description of a family activity that really made them happy and gave them a feeling of closeness to their other family members. They are also asked to write down three things that they admire most about each family member, and three things that really bug them about each family member. Finally, everyone is asked to add the three ways that each family member hurt them in the past. Just stirring the pot!

After the assignment is completed, each person individually reads out loud what he or she has written. A facilitated discussion takes place after each reading. The unspeakables are stirred up and start rising to the top of the pot during this sharing.

For many families, the facilitated discussion is the first time they have ever had an honest, open, in-depth conversation concerning individual feelings and judgments that are often based upon misunderstandings.

Families often avoid the word "love." Because of this, strong positive feelings for each other have never been spoken. Lack or fear of open, honest communication has been the destruction of many family businesses and relationships. Addressing the issues, speaking the unspeakables, being open and honest, loving one another, and voicing personal, often withheld, feelings can have a very positive impact on family members and the business when done in a caring, non-vindictive manner.

THE SCHELL BROTHERS, PART THREE

Jerry, Jim and Dick still get along very well socially. Jerry was not bitter and he did not try to convince Dad to hire him. All the wives got along well and so did the cousins, who acted more like siblings. Jerry had obtained another job, but continued to express his desire to enter the family business. His family relationship was solid and his track record as a successful accountant continued to build. Six months later Jim and Dick, after some soul-searching and discussions with us, realized how immature they were acting. They put together a package, apologized to their brother, as he did to them.

Jerry entered the family business almost seven years ago. His skills and input have been invaluable. His money management is unbelievable and he continues to contribute to the company's bottom-line. The brothers all get along and their father is thankful and proud that his three successful sons are working together well, are growing the business and are extremely respectful of Dad's involvement in the company.

The brothers did it and so can you!

CHAPTER 5

LEARN TO **FORGIVE**

Reframing how a family considers forgiveness

THE JONESES

Joe and Linda Jones, brother and sister, inherited an industrial supply business from their parents, Matt and Donna. Like most families in business, Joe and Linda had been exposed to the company from an early age. They were encouraged to work in each department and to learn as much as they could about all the operations, and they did.

The Dysfunctional

Joe eventually became the president, because he was the boy. Linda was made vice-president and head of sales. Most of the employees felt Linda was the more qualified of the two, but Matt was firm in his belief the company should be run by a man and no other input was asked for or appreciated. Joe grew into the position.

To compensate Linda for this slight, Matt and Donna purchased a home for Linda and gave her a raise so her compensation was the same as Joe's. However, they didn't tell Linda that she was making the same as Matt or that they did not buy him a home. As President, Joe was extremely vocal and bitter when he learned what his Mom and Dad had done for Linda. He believed this was unfair and a major slap in the face in return for the years of hard work and support he had given to his parents and the company. He blamed Matt and Donna for this favoritism and he blamed Linda for not speaking up and supporting him to their parents. He did not know the feelings Linda had about the house or the compensation.

Linda's feelings toward her brother began to turn bitter; his negative attitude and actions towards her became more public and his communication with her became less frequent. This work/family conflict began to create management control and operational problems, as sibling rivalry usually causes confused and uninformed employees to inevitably choose sides.

Joe and Linda's conflict also impacted their relationship with their Mom and Dad because of their feelings of unfairness and lack of support. Joe and Linda serve as an example of a "normal" family working together—there is usually a fight (could be physical) or argument going on. "We're dysfunctional; we are normal."

Stay tuned for the rest of the story.

A wall of hostility builds up between family members when they place blame on one another for all the personal problems and business issues that arise. Righteous rudeness takes the place of open communication. Family members become blame throwers. Emotional reactions pass between family members like electricity between a light and a switch in the blink of an eye. No one in the family will ever completely forget.

The Extraordinary

Families in business who desire to overcome the blame throwing must begin by moving to a state of mind where everyone in the family is treated as an equal. This includes "communicating as equals" and "love for family" as individual commitments. When this takes place, families can get past the emotional and personal issues. They begin to communicate with honesty, trust, and an openness that will enable each issue to be addressed with patience and forgiveness.

Patience allows for a way to open a truthful dialogue based on care and love for one another. The first goal of some of the family members may be the desire to open communication so better decisions can be made in the business. This is usually the first step to better relationships. When communication improves, so do relationships. Either way the result is good for the family as well as the company.

Conflict unaddressed is forgiveness not given. Conflict is a natural part of being a family and especially a family business. Most families in business see "dysfunctional" as normal, but this is not inevitable.

Family members must give up many of the attitudes and mindsets they have towards one another that were usually formed as children. Unfortunately, many family members drag with them into adulthood one or two bad memories about the other family members. Those memories, which develop into the unspeakables we mentioned, become the basis of how they judge the others as adults. These memories can also lead to the desire to get even and prevents them from being willing to forgive.

Family members need to take the time to really get to know one another as adults. To rethink how they may have been hurt by a family member in the past, and to address it, come to a resolution and find a way to forgive and move on. None of us are the same people we were when we were children. Our experiences have helped us grow, good or bad. We have different ways of thinking and acting toward others. Most of the time we do not take the time or effort to learn which experiences of our siblings and other family members have shaped their lives and way of thinking. We assume we know. Our assumptions are not exactly the way things are.

Family members must be able to forgive each other for past hurts. Not forgetting, but giving up the need to get even. When we were children, often the desire was for "pay-back" when a sibling did something we did not like. As adults, we must give up the desire for pay-back and substitute open communication setting aside self-interest, with the goal of finding an agreeable solution. The same is true for the memory baggage we drag around with us. Those memories that impacted us as children remain with us as adults.

THE JONESES, PART TWO

An example of this is a memory Linda has about Joe. When they were children, every time Linda came up with an idea, Joe would say it was stupid and then would punch her in the arm. As they reached adulthood, the physical punching stopped but the memory remained. Linda was reluctant to share her ideas with Joe as she felt he would tell her that her ideas were stupid and he may even punch her! Their business relationship was impacted by a memory and emotion that was still unresolved from childhood.

When confronted by this memory, Joe did not think it was that big of a deal and did not realize the affect it had on how he and his sister communicated today. This added to Linda's frustration and enhanced her negative feelings toward Joe.

Stay tuned for the rest of the story.

This memory is an example of the unspeakables, described in Chapter 4—an issue one or more of the family members know or feel, yet is never discussed. If these are not addressed, they will always hamper communication and trust. A relationship cannot survive when the unspeakables are not addressed. Forgiveness cannot take place and family will always take a back seat to suspicion and mistrust.

KWAISERISM

Forgiving is the positive ingredient in all relationships, for we all make mistakes.

Forgiving and developing or regaining trust is difficult. Forgiving is not the same as forgetting, but it is a step to understanding and redeveloping trust in one another. Trust is necessary in a family business so the right decisions are made, at the right time for the success of the family and the company. Without forgiveness, the relationships will never be as trusting as they should be, and the business will never be as successful as it could be.

Families begin to address these issues by first agreeing to sincerely listen to one another. Next is for the family to commit to work together to find fair solutions to all the issues. Solutions which will allow them to make better business decisions, and allow the family business to be more successful. Emotion must take a back seat to adult communication, common sense and doing what is best for the bigger picture—the family *and* the business. When handled in this manner the outcome will always be beneficial to the business and to each family member.

> ## THE JONESES, PART THREE
>
> Joe and Linda knew they could not continue the way they were. They had to find a way to get past their personal issues or one of them was going to have to leave the business. They decided to ask for help. With professional facilitation the siblings began to think through each issue and logically discuss what was fair, as well as what was best for the company and the family. When Joe and Linda discussed her feelings about Joe not accepting any of her ideas, Joe was surprised and did not realize the impact it had on her life. He sincerely apologized and asked if they could begin again—and they did. After Linda found out that Mom and Dad had bought her a house but not Joe, and she was making the same as Joe, she sat down with him to discuss it. Together they worked out an incentive program where, as President of the company, Joe (or any future president) would participate in the success of the organization. They agreed to meet more frequently and discuss both personal and business issues. Joe and Linda agreed to try this for six months and see what the future could hold. Their relationship and the direction of the company slowly improved.

The Extraordinary

Other Thoughts on Forgiveness

Yes, forgiving is not forgetting. Forgiving has more to do with communicating as adults and finding the solutions that are in the best interest of the family and the business. Forgiving is also not a one-time thing. It is the ability to know quickly when a family member has been hurt or disturbed by something that has been said or done. The issue needs to be addressed immediately, asking the individual affected if he or she is willing to communicate as equal adults, working together to find the right solutions. When personal commitment is combined with humility and brought together, the situation improves.

KWAISERISM

It is never too late to be humble enough to forgive.

Practice This to Help You Forgive

We all know there are several traits that successful leaders and entrepreneurs usually possess. Let's begin with what forgiveness is not. It is...

- Not pride—although pride in one's accomplishments can be a good thing if we realize many of our accomplishments are completed through others.

- Not personal recognition—although we all like to be identified for our successes, if we realize true success comes from giving away credit to those whom we lead.

- Not an overinflated ego—as self-realization is a natural part of being human, if we realize our individual accomplishments can be, at least partially, attributed to those who have shared their knowledge and instruction with us.

The understated trait of forgiveness involves having true modesty about our successes and a true respectfulness to those who have supported us in our accomplishments, along with the realization that we need others. This understanding of forgiveness can result in one of most important traits in a leader, the value of humility.

Consciously practice it—Start today!

CHAPTER 6

LET GO OF THE PECKING ORDER

Change—Are You Kidding?
Moving from avoidance to implementation

Change is going to happen whether we embrace it or not. This is illustrated in the following story: Two caterpillars were crawling across the grass when a butterfly few over them. They looked up, and the one nudged the other and said, "You couldn't get me up in one of those things for a million dollars!"

Change is going to happen to us even when we can't see it coming. Families in business need to embrace change and pass it on to the next generation. If not, like the caterpillars who were not prepared, you will wake up one day and your old world will be gone.

THE CRUSES

"The only one who really likes change is a wet baby!" said creativity guru Roger von Oech.

"If it isn't broke, don't fix it," said sports legend Yogi Berra.

"If it has worked in the past, that's good enough for this family and business."

Bill Cruse used to quote these words of wisdom to his family in their construction service business. This included Bill's wife, Tracy, the Human Resource Manager; his son, Tim, Manager of Research and Development as well as the IT department; and his daughter Anna, the Sales Manager.

Bill's sayings greatly influenced the mindset of his employees, most of whom had been with the company since its founding. Many were complacent and felt that, if they were close to meeting last year's sales, they were doing well. "Everyone knows the economy is bad, so if we are not way behind we are doing ok," was the message sent throughout the company by Bill, so this became the attitude of his people. The employees liked the company, believed that the current pace was the perfect place for the company to be, and this was reinforced by Bill from the top.

Tim tried hard to introduce new products and Anna wanted to expand the business. Bill and many of the employees became the roadblocks to these growth strategies. They knew what they had. The thought of changing the way they did business or moving into different markets was an unknown risk they were not willing to take. Tracy supported her husband, even though she began to see cash declining and payments being stretched. As far as Bill was concerned, things were fine and changes could be made later. They had plenty of time.

Stay tuned for the rest of the story.

The Dysfunctional

A reason many companies do not grow is the lack of extensive financial planning and operational experience among their management team. This lack contributes to their inability to prepare other employees for leadership roles. Without self-learning leaders, and a succession of qualified manager candidates, business growth is going to be an on-going problem

Many times, the fear of change by the owner hampers company growth and longevity. Growth means some change must take place. People can only achieve a certain level of performance and production and cannot reach any higher. This is when change becomes a must for continued success.

Changing a task or separating an individual from the company may become necessary to save the business and protect the security of the family and employees. Companies that experience no growth, or growth from inflation only, are not really growing. They have become stagnant and will eventually erode. This is especially true with family businesses as professional management training and succession planning are rare.

THE CRUSES, PART TWO

The Dysfunctional

Bill was not willing to try anything new. He wanted Tim to spend his time dealing with the IT issues but refused to allow him to implement new systems or methods. "This has always served us well in the past," was Bill's reaction. He seemed to forget the company had tripled in size since the founding and many of the past methods just no longer fit with today's industry.

Many of the employees were at the top of their game and did not know how to grow the company further. Tim was not allowed to develop new systems or services for the company because, "That is not the way we have always done it." Although Anna had developed several relationships and promising prospects in other markets, she was not allowed to develop them because, in Bill's words, "They don't know us there." Many of the employees felt they were overworked now and any more business would "overly task" them. They didn't feel they would be able to handle the load within their present work week.

Bill was afraid to change the way he had run the company for years. He was fearful new suggestions, systems, services and markets would change his company. He was not sure how change would affect the long-term employees who had already voiced a negative attitude toward future company growth.

Bill knew that, no matter what happened, he could survive until retirement. He really did not consider what impact his decision would have on his children. He did not want Tim and Anna to take over the company because he felt they would fundamentally change the way it had been run. He also felt they may let go some long-time employees who were also good friends of his.

Tim and Anna were frustrated as they could not convince their father to make the adjustments necessary to compete in the market. Expanding services, putting in place new processes and product selections, including new items that had been introduced to the industry were all improvements they felt were needed.

Without these changes the growth and future success of the company was suspect, yet they were consistently turned down by their father. They went to their Mother but all she said was, "It's your Father's company and he can do what he wants." There were no conversations about the future or Tim and Anna's roles. There was little discussion about succession or the reasons for Bill's reluctance to make needed changes. Bill listened to his employees, not his family, about the future.

Without everyone making a mindset adjustment, change cannot happen. When it comes to growth, behavior needs to be addressed, but also attitudes toward change and risk.

The Extraordinary

Change happens all around us whether we like it or not. We cannot stop change. We all must continually deal with changes in all aspects of our lives, including the constantly changing dynamics of every industry. As former Vice President Dan Quayle once said, "It's a question of whether we're going forward into the future. Or past to the bank." Yes, that is what he said and I still can't figure it out?!

Dan's words are a good example of how confusing change can be without a system or a process of dealing with it. Change in a family business should include a controlled way of making decisions, trusting advisors and having good common sense when planning tasks. Change includes a re-evaluation of our thinking when it comes to who is the best person for a position or assignment. The old "Pecking Order" just may not be appropriate anymore!

Change isn't necessarily about changing people; but about changing the way tasks are completed, results achieved, and who may be the best person to do the job. Change is a process that needs to be explained to those involved and then followed. Effective change is made up of the following six steps: C.H.A.N.G.E.

1. Communicate with everyone.
2. Have a shared vision of what change will look like in your family business.
3. Allow for discussion, pro and con, on the proposed changes in completing tasks.
4. Never ignore the feelings of others. Never take anything for granted.
5. Get the rules, policies and procedures in place for what change is and how to handle each one.
6. Evaluate each task change monthly.

KWAISERISM

If you want to succeed, you can either try to work harder or you can find a different way of doing things, by changing.

These change steps are an important part of moving from "normal/dysfunctional" to "extraordinary" within a family business. When they are not followed, committed to and communicated to all family members, a feeling of mistrust develops.

A lack of trust within a family will always lead to suspicion of the motives of family members. Proper communication of change, focusing on changing processes and not people, and having family members and other employees involved from the beginning, will set the stage for needed change in the future and ensure more success for implementation of any new process. Communication, or lack of it, plays the most important role in success or failure as a family business and with family relationships.

> ## THE CRUSES, PART THREE
>
> Tim and Anna began to realize their father was not going to grow the business and there would be no future for them, unless his attitude changed. The siblings and their spouses came together, planned, and then met with Bill and Tracy.
>
> They explained they loved working in the business and felt it was their future, but without growth their chances of success were greatly diminished. They asked their father, "What do you need to feel secure in retirement?"
>
> The family came to an agreement to buy-out Bill, allowing him to be a consultant to the company with defined guidelines, including rewards and penalties. They made key personnel changes to help them with operations and, with other employees, put together a strategic plan that they all agreed to and are promoting. At this point, we don't know how successful Tim and Anna will be, but with the support they now have and the process changes being implemented, their future and security for their employees looks much more promising.

Other Thoughts on Change

Many people are what I call "rut runners." They may not like the way things are, but they know where they are. They can survive in the rut because they have been there so long they think they know what

KWAISERISM

In a family you can be ugly, lack common sense, do stupid things, and still be loved.

In a business, you can only be ugly.

lies ahead. They are afraid to come up out of the rut, because they do not know what is up there. Whether good, or bad, they are not willing to take the risk of change. They will stay in the rut, not improving their state in life, due to the fear of change. So, they wait. Change will come and they will not be prepared. They will stay in the rut as it has become less scary than promoting change.

Change is inevitable. Most people view change like death and taxes - to be avoided.

Some believe change is going to cost them too much. Convinced there will be a disruption of what they have been comfortable with, even if the current situation is not in the best interest of the company or employees, is a disruption they are unwilling to take.

They are correct, disruption will take place. "Normal/dysfunctional" disruption. With change, people never really know the result until it is implemented. The certainty of change, even good change, becomes scary, risky and even emotionally stressful and painful. Rarely are these emotions discussed, as most adults don't like to admit change is scary. They don't want to be perceived as weak or afraid, so they put change off if possible.

"It is not the strongest of the species that survive, nor the most intelligent, but the one most responsive to change." – Charles Darwin

Thoughts on Reluctance and Change

Most senior generation family business owners are reluctant to "pass the baton" to the next generation, to let go. This was verified in a study compiled by Price Waterhouse who dubbed this the "sticky baton syndrome."

We have experienced several senior generation members who want to let go but are stuck with the realization the next generation will not do things exactly the way they have. Most are also stuck with their own inability to plan for the days when they will no longer work full-time in the business, so they hold on a little tighter. Many owners use apparently logical reasons as excuses to remain glued to the family business. Many of those reasons are disputed by the next generation who are ready to take the reins and anxious to make their own mark.

Families in business must accept that each succeeding generation will do things differently than the previous one. Change is a part of life in the business cycle and with each family in business. New technologies, new ways of marketing and merchandising, new products and new store fronts will be just a few of the changes that will happen in the next generation's re-creation of the business. "The sticky baton" syndrome often delays this re-creation process, hinders growth, and can even contribute to the failure of succeeding generations.

Now is the time to review your family business for any signs of the "sticky baton syndrome." Take a realistic look at what the next phase of your family business should be for you. Prepare to be the best coach and mentor as a member of the senior generation, and the best performance leader as a member of the succeeding generation. Without this preparation, the next generation tries to grab the baton too quickly from hands that are tightly glued to it. No one wins and the family loses.

Get the help you need. Listen to advice from professionals and as a family decide the right direction for your business, then make a plan that is fair, realistic and achievable. Anything less may make it impossible to ever let go and for the next generation to ever really be ready to take over.

THE SEMANS

Fred and Thresa Semans owned a successful lumber business. They have three children—Saul, Stephen and Susan.

From the time his oldest son, Saul, was small, Fred spent most of his time preparing him to become chairman of the board of the family business.

Saul was exposed early on to the business and began working in various capacities as soon as he was old enough. Fred moved him from position to position, telling him war stories and allowing him to experience all types of leadership and decision-making situations.

Eventually Fred introduced Saul to the industry by having him join the right professional organizations, allowing him to represent the company at public functions, and placing him on the board of directors of the business. Fred would proudly say, "My oldest son will take over the business. He will be in charge when I am finally carried out of here." Fred was also proud of following the right "pecking order," as his father had before him.

The Dysfunctional

Fred felt he was doing the right thing, setting the right stage, and properly planning for the future of his company. There was only one thing he did not plan on. Saul was tragically killed in a boating accident at the age of 27.

Stephen and Susan were not trained to run the business and they were bitter about not being involved. Although they loved their older brother, they always felt inferior. They had never really been allowed to make decisions, gain business experience, or hear the war stories that Saul had. They were not communicated with or listened to. Their opinions had not mattered in the past, and their attitude toward work and the business reflected this. They were not prepared to become decision makers in the company.

Fred was getting older and wanted to reduce his work load. He tried to communicate to Stephen and Susan all the lessons that had been reserved for Saul. He was angry his oldest son had died. He took out his anger, sorrow, and frustration on the other children.

Fred was not a patient communicator. He would not *communicate with them as equals*. He did not *share the vision* with them. He refused to *address the unspeakables*. Worst of all, he would not *let go of the pecking order*.

Fred decided to force his second oldest son, Stephen, into becoming the next heir apparent.

Stephen was now pushed into a business he did not like, in a position he did not want, making decisions he was not qualified to make. He was not capable of running the company.

However, his younger sister Susan was. She had the business savvy, had studied the industry, and had kept herself up-to-date on the financial and operational condition of the company. Fred would not teach, coach, or communicate with her, as she was not the next son in line.

Because of this refusal to *let go of the pecking order*, Fred brought in two non-family members to run the company and mentor Stephen. Bitterness grew. Susan left the company due to her father's inability to communicate with her as an equal, his inability to share his vision, their combined inability to address the unspeakables, and finally, his refusal to let go of the pecking order.

The non-family members fought for control and the business deteriorated. Market share declined, customers jumped ship, and many experienced managers left for greener pastures because of

> Fred's poor communication skills and his adherence to what he deemed to be the proper pecking order.

The Extraordinary

To be able to let go of the pecking order, owners of family businesses need to look more at the rate of learning, the skills learned and the behaviour of their children. The pecking order has to take a back seat to ability when it comes to running the business. Sure, some favoritism in the perks and pay may occur, but the children must be given the same learning and ability considerations as other employees.

When they are ready, their behavioral styles need to be assessed to establish a plan for them to increase their effectiveness. Particular jobs for them need to be identified, with defined, written job descriptions. The children should be allowed to work together and with other people who can teach them. This will enable the family members to gain respect for one another by working together and reporting on their progress. It will also help in evaluating the next leader. Be sure to communicate with all the children about the business—do not show favoritism.

Openness of communication, love, and forgiveness will all play a role in who will eventually lead the business. The child with the best overall skills should be the next to run the company and that person just may not be the oldest boy.

CHAPTER 7

EXPAND YOUR ADVISORS

No, you can't do it alone
Making use of the right people

A father was ploughing a field and his son was going ahead of him, moving the stones out of the way. Everything stopped when the boy was not able to move a very large stone. The father asked his son, "Did you use all of your strength to move the stone?" The son said yes. The father replied, "No, you didn't, as you did not ask me to help you."

Unfortunately, this story applies to many families in business. The senior members won't ask anyone for help, not only with succession and estate planning, but also with personal family issues. Often, they pass up the needed professional help because of family pride and a desire to not air their dirty laundry. The succeeding generations are like the son in the preceding story. They won't ask for help from the senior generation, and they continue to try it on their own even when help is available.

THE FLOWERS

The Dysfunctional

Reece and Cindy Flowers owned a car dealership. They had two sons in the business, Trent and Albert, as well as a daughter Candice. The company was barely holding its own; cash was tight.

Reece was a strict boss which carried over into their home lives as well. Reece and Trent rarely spoke as Trent felt his Dad never listened and did not want any input. Making suggestions would be as a waste of time. Reece felt Trent was disrespectful and not as productive as he should be. Albert and Candice tried to stay out of the fights and disagreements so they did whatever Dad told them and kept their eyes and ears open for other opportunities.

Cindy, although she knew all her children's complaints were valid, would not go head to head with Reece over any issue that was not her own. This was unfortunate as spouses are usually the best advisors entrepreneurs can have. They take on the role of the straight-talking, loving partner who always explains to the main entrepreneur what he needs to hear and not just what he wants to hear. This should happen in private, away from employees and other family members, as the couple should always be of a unified mind when addressing a family business situation.

Reece and Cindy wanted to begin the process of succession planning and make some operational changes. Reece felt he could do this on his own. The couple did not want anyone else to know about the inter-family conflict or how close the company was to being insolvent, so they refused to seek help. Both the business and family relationships continued to erode.

Families are always complex. The Flowers family members have different ideas, thoughts and opinions on just about everything. One of the biggest failings of family business owners centers on pride. They see the company as another child they gave birth to, and no one is going to tell them how to handle their child, even the other children.

Reece and Cindy wanted to begin the process of succession, but were reluctant because they didn't know how to start and did not want to admit their lack of knowledge. They felt this would be a sign of weakness to their family or professional advisors. Like other families, they were going to wait until things changed.

But unless the family is willing to change they never do. Reece and Cindy didn't want to admit they are getting older and are no longer interested in putting in the same effort as they did when they started. They also do not want to admit the business is faltering; if this continues there will not be enough left to support the next generation. The sad fact is that there is plenty of help available. Unfortunately, like so many others, Reece and Cindy did not want to, or just didn't know how to, work with and take advantage of the professional advice and assistance available.

The Extraordinary

The first challenge the Flowers family must deal with is the success or failure of the business as they also deal with the conflict between Trent and Reece. An upswing in the company could give their children hope for the future.

Stay tuned for the rest of the story.

One of the best ways to begin is to contact an independent advisor who will always act on your behalf. Your current professional advisors—accountants, lawyers—have their companies to worry about and will want to move you to a place that is beneficial for them. As we have assisted the family businesses identified in this book, an independent advisor/consultant can help you objectively and consult with you on a variety of issues.

A family business advisor sits with you and ensures that you are getting the information you need from other advisors. He or she can walk you effectively through succession as well as the operations of your company, acting as a guide and a sounding block for your operational development. This type of advisor can help you to understand and facilitate the personal and emotional issues that must be brought out and resolved. Another area this professional can assist with is the selection and development of a board of advisors (or, when appropriate, board of directors) for your company.

A board of advisors will bring an objective view of the conflicts between family members. Families in business who practice open, honest communication, and have trust for one another, can often face and resolve potential problems. But not always. Even with all those positive traits present, the family must remain sensitive to potential conflicts. A board of advisors can be a real asset when objectively considering these issues.

A board of advisors does not have fiduciary responsibility to the company, so liability insurance on the advisors is not required. Even without legal responsibility, the advisors certainly can be asked to hold the owners accountable for the success of the company and for the development and implementation of a succession plan. They can help grow a company with suggestions and innovative ideas as well as shore up the ownership in areas of potential weakness.

For example, owners who do not have a strong financial background can make sure they have a person on their board who does. This individual can also teach the working family members more about watching the numbers and how to use them to make decisions. If sales are a problem, a strong successful individual who has a good sales background can be appointed.

We suggest having three non-family members on the board of advisors; the total number should always be odd to avoid tie votes.

They should *not* be your accountant, banker, lawyer, financial advisor or insurance broker. These people are already your advisors and they can be brought into meetings as needed. Also, there may come a time to change your accountant, banker, etc. and if they are on the board that could be a potential problem. The board member does not have to be a professional in your business. The most crucial factor is that the individual has been very involved—preferably as an owner—in a family business, is successful, understands the business of business, and has a strong desire to help.

The use of non-family board members can reduce the number of decisions made based purely on emotion. This board structure allows for more communication as equals, while helping to minimize the side-tracking of critical issues.

Non-family board members are not needed in every family business. Families who practice honest, open communication, trust, and forgiveness as key ingredients in their relationships can usually face and resolve potential differences. Even with these traits, the parents need to remain sensitive to the relationships of their children and consider non-family board members if relationships deteriorate. The board of directors should always be expanded to include the adult children who will inherit the business, whether or not outside board members are involved.

The selection of outside advisors should be discussed with family members at a scheduled business meeting. Each family member should propose possible candidates for the board. The prospective members should be reviewed, their qualifications discussed, and the list shortened to five prospects. Those candidates should be approached and asked if they would be willing to serve in this role. If there is interest from the prospects, they should be interviewed by the entire family. All members must agree on the selections.

KWAISERISM

Without family, whatever that definition is for you, you are truly alone.

All board members should be evaluated individually—for their effectiveness, opinions, and decision-making skills for the benefit of the entire family and the business—by the other members of the board.

A board of advisors meet at least four times a year. When you first start out we recommend meeting once a month so the board can gain a better understanding of your business. They should get to know your working family members and they can even be used as mentors to the next generation.

The board of advisors should be paid—although not as much as a board of directors—for each meeting attended.

Board members should have job descriptions that include areas in which they can help the family overcome deadlocked decisions. They can also assist with inter-family conflict by being more objective than family members, on personal and business issues. They will also have a more objective view of the status of the company. Identifying the roles and duties of the board, on both personal and business issues, and utilizing non-family board members, can help the family reduce potential conflict. issues like compensation, perks, position, and title, that arise due to lack of trust within the family. Appropriate members should participate in constructing the job description for the board as part of their initial responsibilities. Having written job descriptions for the members of the board will give family members a better understanding of the authority of the board and its relationship to the president and chief operating officer of the company. This document will also define for the non-family board members what will be expected of them.

Understanding the authority of the board of directors can soften the blow to those who may be disappointed they were not elected president. The authority of the board includes setting the company direction, which is then given to the president, who carries it out. A clear explanation of the authority of the board allows all family members to understand that, as board members, they are very much a part of the decision-making process of the company. The board can develop or review job descriptions for the other key positions in the company.

Some suggested duties for the board of directors include:

1. Declare dividends;
2. Elect officers;
3. Approve the budget;
4. Approve all acquisitions, expansions, etc.;
5. Approve major equipment purchases;
6. Approve company objectives, business plans, finances, and the philosophy statement for the company;
7. Approve salaries of key employees;
8. Approve bonuses to key employees;
9. Determine how family members enter or leave the business;
10. Complete performance evaluations of board members.

A good board of advisors will be there because they want to be and not for the money. They will help you see things in your business you have not seen before. They will bring new ideas and new eyes to your company, products and marketplace. They will be an important factor in helping your family and family business move to "Extraordinary"!

Having your working family members on your board will open even wider communication between all family members. They will learn together, know each other from a business perspective, and begin to better understand what is involved in running a family business, not just working in one.

The board of directors or advisors meeting becomes a safe place to address certain issues and to give feedback some family members would not feel comfortable giving in a work environment. When families are more involved in the business, the business improves, and usually the relationships do as well. You do not have to be alone in making decisions. Most family members who work in the company see the company as theirs, whether they have ownership or not. Having a voice makes them even more committed to the family and the business.

THE FLOWERS, PART TWO

Reece, however, decided to try to do it on his own. While Cindy thought that getting some help was the best option, Reece felt that he could handle the issues by himself.

He could not. Trent eventually left the company. He saw no change coming from his Dad and he did not want to work in that environment any more. He is now working for a competitor in another state and could become a partial owner.

> Candice recently got married and is now working part-time in the business. Albert is still in the family business, but is in conversation with Trent about coming to work with him. The opportunity could be for both to eventually own this out of state dealership, a competitor.
>
> Reece is now working harder than ever. He lost his top sales person; Candice has gone to part-time; Albert is doing the best he can, but his heart is no longer in his Dad's business. Reece did not get outside help, never did a succession plan, never held himself accountable to anyone, and could not accept that his adult children were just as concerned about the business as he was. He never acknowledged that they had thoughts and ideas that may have helped him.
>
> Like our story about the farmer's son who was trying to move the rock, Reece did not use all his resources. He was trying to move his business and personal rocks and he did not use all his strength. He did not ask for help from his family. We could say that Reece was just "normal."

Most parents have never communicated the importance of having advisors or asking for outside help with their children, and the children end up failing as successors due to this lack of advisors. Teach your children to recognize who their best advisors really are.

Never downplay the importance of advisors. Make sure you recognize who your advisors were when you started, and who the important ones are now. Communicate to your children the impact they have had on your success. The successors may not have the same advisors, so you will need to guide them in selecting new ones. Teach your business heirs to recognize the important qualities, expertise, and experience advisors can bring.

Adult children need to understand that they cannot operate a successful, profitable business alone. Having experienced, qualified, trusted advisors, while not insuring success, certainly helps reduce the chance of failure. As stated in the book of Proverbs 15:22 "Plans fail for lack of counsel." An effective board of directors can help solve that problem.

Other Thoughts on Advice

Having extended family meetings is another way to include others and receive outside input. A full, family update meeting with spouses, children etc. should happen once a year. This meeting is not held to get their approval. The purpose is to inform them how the company is doing, and what opportunities may be available to them. The meeting is also structured to elicit any suggestions they may have for the betterment of the family business.

You would be surprised at the number of extraordinary suggestions that will eventually come from these meetings. You should have an agenda and involve the working family members in the presentation. Doing this before a meal is a great get together for families. Families meeting around food are usually more open and receptive.

Most families in business can't do it alone and they don't need to. In addition to the professionals mentioned, there are consultants in all competencies related to family business, covering everything from sales, to budgeting, to finance, to effectively addressing the personal and emotional issues of succession planning, including preparing and completing a succession plan. There is a lot of help; a family in business just has to take that first step. The right time is now, yet many go it alone.

I get a kick out of being told by members of family businesses they can't afford to get help. Yet they often spend thousands of dollars on yearly golf outings or shopping sprees or going to a convention because they like the location! They think they can spend the money on these things, and won't give them up for a short period to invest those same dollars into their family and the growth of their business. An investment now in the family and the future will return a lot more than one outing.

You could take your company from the normal/dysfunctional to the extraordinary. Which is more important to you?

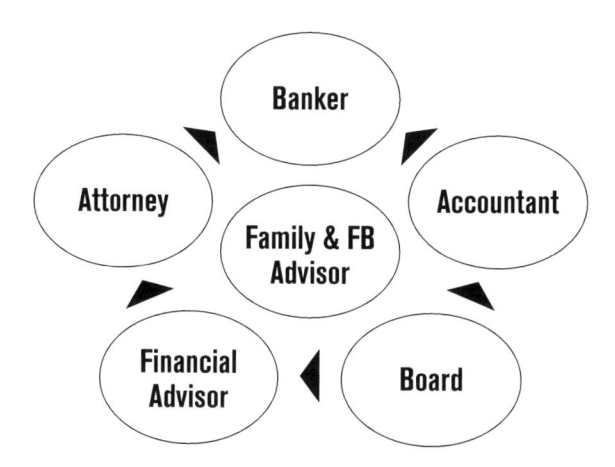

```
         Banker
  Attorney    Accountant
      Family & FB
        Advisor
  Financial     Board
   Advisor
```

Remember—your greatest advisor is your spouse! He or she is your partner in all aspects of your life. Don't shut him or her out of the area where you spend most of your time. Do you pass things by your spouse before you make decisions? "But she doesn't know anything about the company" is not a good excuse.

Spouses' questions can stimulate a new thought, idea or even a *solution!* Remember, who may be running the business if you become disabled or die. Your spouse may be the individual who will be coaching your next generation into the business. Keep him or her in the loop as to your thoughts and plans. This is another good reason for a qualified board of advisors to assist you.

Other Thoughts on Support of a Spouse

Most entrepreneurs would not be in business without the help and support of their spouses. The spouse is often the partner as well as the only other employee when the business is founded.

As the business grows and more family members enter, often the spouse's role in the founding and initial success of the business is forgotten or not completely appreciated by the next generation. When this happens, the spouse may be viewed as either not being a part of the company or as just another employee. He or she may not be given respect or acknowledged as a partner, owner or key manager/advisor in the business.

Don't forget to inform other family members of the key role your spouse had in starting the business, including putting everything on the line—to help and support the business by having to sign loan documents with many of their possessions as collateral. The spouse's role is part of the history and make-up of the company and should be emphasized to the next generation.

In the next generation, working family members often use their own spouses as a sounding board. Unfortunately, the "sounding" is usually complaining about other family members they work with. After constantly hearing about the on-going problems of working with family members, the spouse can sometimes form a negative attitude and tainted view of their in-laws. Don't forget to tell your spouse about the positive aspects of working with your family, especially when a problem has been resolved. Be sure to let him or her know when you are the one who made the mistake or that your attitude may have caused the problem. Don't forget to tell your spouse the whole story and not just your emotional response. Truthfulness in your role in creating problems can go a long way towards maintaining family harmony.

Having a meeting at least a once a year with all your family members and their spouses can be helpful in everyone's understanding of the family relationships. Many times, spouses are surprised at how well the family members get along. All they have heard about is how bad working with the family can be! With open and honest communication, your spouse is the best advisor you can have. He or she should be your *first* advisor. Don't forget to seek out opinions, be grateful for input and—be sure to say "I love you." This makes life that much more enjoyable!

CHAPTER 8

NEVER DICTATE

Dictatorship or leadership?
Hindering innovation and creativity

THE RODGERS

Tony and Jennifer Rodgers worked hard all their lives. They had purchased a small tool shop early in their marriage. Tony told anyone who asked that he bought the tool shop "Because I had to do something to put food on the table and I really can't work for anyone else."

Tony handled the operations and Jennifer took care of the financial side. They have two sons, AJ and Doug, who grew up in the tool business. From the time they were small they had been exposed to the business and were expected to do their fair share for their age. As they matured they were expected to gain business knowledge and contribute more to the success of the business.

The Dysfunctional

Tony, a tough task-master, believed as the owner and the father, what he stated was law to be followed without question. He rarely asked for Jennifer's opinions; his communication consisted of telling others what they needed to do, and he rarely carried on a regular conversation. Usually in a hurry to get things done, he never explained his decisions. Most of the time he just yelled out his orders and expected his sons and employees to follow them without question.

Tony tried to run the business by the same family rules he had been raised on. This included the unspoken—and many times spoken-rule that dad talks and everyone else listens and does what he says. He was never to be questioned.

Tony believed to ask for help from others was a sign of weakness. He rejected other opinions and never asked for assistance. Tony would blow up if people had to be told to help others as he felt that this showed a lack of teamwork and was a sign of disrespect.

Tony believed in internal competition and wanted his sons to demonstrate which one would contribute more to the company than the other. Tony's need to be in charge kept him from allowing his sons to individually shine. As a result, sibling competition slowly turned to jealousy. Soon the brothers turned against one another.

Tony continued to place AJ and Doug in competitive situations where one would win and one would lose. He would point out examples: How well they did at sports in school. How many sales each made at the shop. How much money each brought in with every order. The one who did the best was given the greatest attention and the one who came in second was basically ignored.

As time went on, AJ received the most praise. Doug, while he succeeded at sports and was good at sales, never quite reached the results of AJ, and so received little if any praise for his accomplishments. Tony's reaction was to push AJ to try harder—

even his successes were not good enough—and for Doug to become more like his brother.

Tony continued to put into place his arbitrary rules that increased the competition between AJ and Doug. This ended up splitting the work force into two camps; those who liked Doug's more laid back style and those who followed AJ's "get it done at any cost" attitude.

Even though Tony was hard on his family, he believed the business should be able to take care of their needs. While his theory may be correct, his implementation wasn't.

AJ lived at home while Doug and his new wife Ann had just purchased a home. Although AJ was the company's top producer, Doug made more money because he was married with responsibilities. In Tony's eyes, AJ really did not have any.

AJ resented that Doug was making more than he was, and Doug resented that AJ got all the accolades. AJ and Doug's relationship, while close when they were younger, had deteriorated to the point where they no longer socialized and rarely spoke, even at work. While Tony did meet with both his sons occasionally, he mostly gave instruction rather than informing, discussing or agreeing on results. His sons really were not informed about the direction of the business until after decisions had been made. Then Dad would assign them to follow through on what he had instituted.

This process increased AJ's and Doug's animosity towards their father to the point where all three were making decisions independent of one another. This decision-making crisis caused a strain on inventory and cash-flow as well as family relationships.

These strained relationships spread to the in-laws. When Doug went home to his wife, Ann, he would complain about work, mostly about his father and brother; he constantly told her how unfair he was being treated by both.

As a loving wife, Ann viewed her husband as a victim of an unfair father and a leech of a brother. She wanted nothing to do with Doug's family and used every excuse possible not to be a part of family gatherings. Ann had never been involved in a family meeting. She really didn't know what her husband did and had no idea of what the future held for her or Doug. She only knew that her husband was unhappy and because of that she regularly encouraged him to quit and find another place to work. Jennifer, Tony's wife, was at the end of her rope. She viewed her family breaking apart but saw no way to fix it. She knew that her sons were no longer close and did not respect or confide in one another. Tony would come home from work and complain about how lazy AJ and Doug were. "They will never do the job," he would constantly say.

At the dinner table, she was tired of AJ and Tony getting into yelling matches about work. She worried that if something happened to Tony the boys would not have the benefit of their dad's instruction in the "business of business" and would be unprepared to take over. They would be in the dark as far as dealing with vendors and banks, pricing product, and managing the operational side of the business.

Jennifer was also concerned about the future of the family relationships. Ann had announced, by Facebook, that she and Doug were pregnant. Because of their relationship and the lack of family communication, Jennifer worried that she would never be close to her daughter-in-law and maybe never have a close relationship with her first grandchild.

She rarely saw Doug and when she did it was usually without Ann. Jennifer was tired of the business coming before the family. She was tired of Tony repeatedly telling her that without the business she would have nothing. To Tony, the business had to come before anything else, including the family. Tony claimed there was plenty of time to figure out what would happen in the future, and the boys would eventually work it out on their own.

Jennifer had given up fighting with Tony as he ignored her concerns and had not made any changes in the way he operated the business or dealt with their sons or the employees.

AJ and Doug were also fed up. Neither was sure exactly what they were supposed to be doing, what they were responsible for, or how much authority each had. Individually they had been questioning their Dad about future ownership including when, and if, they were going to own the company. Tony put them off. He continually told them they had a lot to learn and a long way to go before they would ever be able to fill his shoes.

The business fell into a downturn. The boys were not as enthusiastic about the business as they once were. Communication between family members had not improved. There was a lack of respect and trust for one another. The family did not work as a team and their relationships were seriously damaged.

Stay tuned for the rest of the story.

Unfortunately, many of these issues have become the definition of "normal" for many families in business. This verifies the statement, "Our family is normal, we're dysfunctional." This applies to far too many dysfunctional families in business.

The Extraordinary

All families in business are confronted by tough times and personal challenges. When this takes place, two choices can be made: First, keep doing what they are doing. Refuse to drop their defenses or work as a team. Continue to see one another as enemies. Like the Rodgers, each can refuse to listen to one another, and believe only their opinion matters. They argue, yell and villainize one another.

A dictator is running the company and the family. They see others as the center of all problems with statements like, "If only my family members would shape up, we would be a better family and better company." This is truly a no-win alternative and will not be understood until the family splits and the business closes or is sold. The family will never truly be a family. They are "normal" by being dysfunctional.

The second choice begins with a conscious self-review by everyone:

- How do I treat the others?
- Do I listen to their opinions with an open mind and open heart?
- Am I truly concerned about each family member's success and happiness?
- Will I let go of the past and try to leave behind all that is negative and critical?
- Will I be positive and reaffirming to bring the family together as a cohesive unit, caring for one another and working together for the best interest of the family and the business?
- Am I willing to forgive my perceived injustices of the past to take a chance at repairing family hurts?
- Am I willing to take the first step in making the change no matter what walls are placed in front of me?

Patience needs to be practiced repeatedly. Set limits; there must be a timetable to end the disruption, the normal dysfunction and the trickiness of over-blown egos.

Patience must have boundaries. When it doesn't, the family will always be held hostage by one self-serving family member who may never see the value of the others. The miracle that overcomes family dysfunction begins with you.

> ## THE RODGERS, PART TWO
>
> With our intervention, AJ and Doug began to realize their futures depended upon one another. They decided to finally sit down and openly talk to one another. AJ had not realized Doug was constantly put down and Doug had not realized he was making more than AJ.
>
> They are talking more now, and AJ has been over to Doug's home where he and Ann are moving closer to a true brother and sister-in-law relationship. Ann has asked AJ to be the godfather to their son. The brothers are working on a plan to present to their Dad. They are working in a unified manner, beginning by stating how much they love and respect their father.
>
> They believe they can have more patience. They will determine what they need to do to change for the better before they ask their Dad to make the changes.
>
> Jennifer has become closer to Ann and she has taken a stronger position with Tony over the need for proper implementation of succession planning, including better treatment of AJ and Doug.
>
> The Rodgers all do love one another. If they keep the love of family in front of every conversation, every plan, they will turn

> away from being a "normal, dysfunctional family" and experience the results "extraordinary" can produce.
>
> ## Other Thoughts on Dictatorships
>
> Pure dictatorships do not work in a family business. Leaders must make a conscious decision to show respect for others, to give and keep the trust of family members, customers and vendors. Family business leaders must be committed to determine and then implement steps to keep the family united and the business successful. Tony is slowly beginning to understand this commitment.

Being sensitive to the feelings of all family members and making their problems your problems is part of the long-term success of family business leaders. Cooperative management in a family business is the most effective way to teach, coach and grow your business for the next generation.

Dictators usually don't want others to get credit for any business success. They take the credit and rule by fear. Forget how much you own or how you started the business; view and treat all family members as owners or potential owners. Most family members want to be a part of the success of the company. Treat them as partners and adults who deserve respect and they may act more like partners!

Using Meetings to Rein in a Dictatorship

One of the surest ways of creating mistrust in a family business is for either the parents or one of the adult children to dictate to the rest of the family what needs to be done. Dictating solutions dissipates communication as equals and the unspeakables build up.

The best way to overcome a family member's tendency to dictate solutions is by having regularly scheduled business meetings. Previously we discussed the importance of meetings as an effective method to communicate as equals. They are also the most effective way to reach consensus.

Meetings must be planned. Prior to the meeting, each participant should submit to the president any items they wish to be addressed. These should be included on the written agenda.

The company president should chair the meeting and be strong enough to keep the discussion focused on the agenda topics. Every family member involved in the business, plus other key employees, should be present. The meeting should take no longer than two hours, starting and ending on time.

Held at least every two weeks, these meetings will help keep all high-level business participants informed and eliminate the feeling that one family member is dictating to the others.

KWAISERISM

Dictators instill fear.

Fear is not desirable in a family or business.

KWAISERISM

Not everyone needs to be in every meeting.

Don't waste people's times in unproductive meetings—

It will cost you every time.

Another successful communication tool involves separate family meetings to address hurt feelings or misunderstandings that can cloud judgment and damage the business. Preparation is a vital component for these meetings as well, including an agenda that addresses personal issues and a timetable. The role of chairperson should rotate throughout the family.

Treat these separate communication meetings as vital, important, and as necessary to the business as meetings with vendors, accountants, or bankers. If separate family-only meetings are treated as unimportant, family members will place them low on their list of priorities. When that happens, communication can revert to the old techniques that build conflict.

When conflict exists among family members, these once a month family meetings can help heal relationships. Everybody gets five minutes to bring up anything on their mind. The topic does not have to relate to business; maybe the previous week's personal activities need to be discussed. The chairperson is charged with monitoring everyone's sharing time. If someone has a serious situation to discuss, a consensus vote can suspend other comments and address the one issue.

These meetings need to have flexible rules, yet be structured enough to avoid becoming gripe sessions. The family meeting works well as a forum to address, discuss and resolve the unspeakables. The first few meetings may need to be facilitated by a non-family member to help make the time productive and start the process of resolving conflict.

Families we have worked with have found these meetings to be an invaluable tool in reintroducing family members to each other. The meetings also enable family members to focus on each other as family members instead of competitors or just fellow employees. When relationships improve, so does communication and decision making. Issues that are addressed by the entire family, with the good of every family member as the focus, will give rise to the proper solutions.

CHAPTER 9

GET YOUR PRIORITIES STRAIGHT

FAMILY FIRST—Really?
Re-creating the priorities of a family business

My wife and I were recently taking a parking shuttle to the airport. As we got off, an attractive woman who was on the shuttle with us, approached my wife, gently placed her hand on my wife's arm and said, "Enjoy traveling with your husband as the time together is very short. I lost my husband a year ago, today." The woman and my wife embraced and she hurried off to catch her plane.

How many times do we allow other things, including business, to get in the way of placing those we love, our family, first? Many family business advisors and other professionals strongly recommend that the family issues be totally separate from the business. When this happens, either the family or the business is short-changed.

In a family business, personal and business cannot be separated. They are interconnected and one does affect the other. Have you ever been upset by your spouse and had this affect you for the first few hours at work? Have you ever had an employee come into work upset because something bad happened at home? Anything from a personal issue with a family member, to a dying pet. Will this affect their performance for a few hours or maybe the entire day? Of course! In a business where family members work together, an argument or family issue can disrupt the work day for everyone.

THE WALLERS

Ralph and Nancy Waller have four siblings working in their concrete business. Two sons, Derek and Frank and two daughters, Patti and Adrianne. Patti, the eldest daughter was made president by Dad and initially there were no questions or concerns about her holding the position. Everyone agreed that she was qualified and did well leading the company.

The Dysfunctional

As time went on, Frank, the second eldest, began to believe that he should have a larger role. As the oldest son, he felt that he should be the president and established as head of the family and the business.

While there were rules that all had agreed to, Frank could no longer commit to the agreement because of his feelings concerning his sister's position as president. Employees sensed the strain (they always do!) and productivity was affected.

The Extraordinary

The family came together, asked for our help and, out of care, love and concern for one another, addressed the issue in an open, mature way.

After several meetings and emotional conversations, all the Wallers understood Frank needed to feel he was in control, but that this could not happen in their family business. Frank decided to search for another job. The family supported him in this, allowed him to keep his stock in the company (converting them to non-voting shares) and after completing

> due diligence, assisted him by financing him in another business. Frank was told that if he ever wanted to come back, the door would always be open, if he would fully support their agreements.
>
> The Wallers had worked together for a solution that was the right fit for the entire family. Thus, the relationships are still strong, Frank is now President of a start-up company and the Waller family business is again flourishing. The distraction of rivalry is no longer present.
>
> The family could have fired Frank and let him go out on his own. Instead they recognized the problem and, by working together, found a solution that was in his best interest *and* the best interest of the family. They did not throw away their brother. They saw his concern, not as an emotional rant, but as a problem for him that became their problem. Frank became a major concern of the family and they came together and properly addressed it. They definitely had their priorities right!

What a great example of FAMILY FIRST: Taking seriously an issue that is of concern to another family member, even if all the family doesn't agree, and coming together to find a solution—this has proven to be in everyone's best interest.

Personal and business cannot be successfully separated in a family business. Learning how to blend them is what helps families in business retain and strengthen relationships and grow their business from generation to generation. If families don't work on their family relationships and deal with the inevitable emotional issues, they lose interest in continuing the businesses due to the inter-family stress.

Less than one-third of family businesses make it through the second generation. Less than 5% enter the fourth generation.

From our experience in working with hundreds of family businesses, the failures took place when families tried to separate the personal from the business and ignored the emotions of family members.

THE GENOS

The Dysfunctional

The Geno family had a very successful, international canning company. Fred, the patriarch, was a strong believer in separation of family and business. He knew of many family businesses that failed due to the personal issues that got in the way. He was going to be sure it never happened to his business.

Each of his sons, Hunter, Grayson and Charles had a clear job description so no one stepped on another's toes. Fred also physically separated them from one another. Fred stationed each in different states and even different countries so that they, in his opinion, would not be in conflict. They reported directly to him and he coordinated the times when they would all meet.

Fred was also concerned about in-law conflict, so he encouraged his sons to not socialize with one another. The only time the family came together was once a year at Thanksgiving. While well-intentioned, this is certainly not an example of family before business. Future generations won't know one another and yet may end up being business owners together. A great recipe for future generation failure.

Stay tuned for the rest of the story.

The Extraordinary

The following are the major ingredients to establishing the right priorities for the FAMILY FIRST philosophy:

1. As a family, develop a Family Code of Conduct, in writing.
2. Get to know one another better as adults; not just as the siblings you grew up with and remember as kids, and not just the parents you rarely shared real opinions with.
3. *Never* talk against one another to anyone, in or outside the family or business.
4. Never allow anyone to say something against another family member.
5. Talk to one another on a regularly scheduled basis about the business.
6. *Know when to apologize!*
7. Respect the different traits in your family members.
8. Respect what others are doing.
9. Trust that your family members working in the business have the right motive for the decisions they make.
10. Act as if all family members working in the business are owners for discussion of decisions, direction and blending of the family and business culture.
11. Communicate all agreements of the working family members to the extended family.
12. FAMILY FIRST is about love of the family. Years ago, one of my clients told me an acronym for FAMILY:

FORGETTING ABOUT ME IS LOVING YOU

These ingredients move families and family businesses to the extraordinary.

When the business is placed before family, the family loses its cohesive love of one another. You just become people who happen to share the same last name.

"Love doesn't just sit there, like a stone, it has to be made, like bread, remade all the time, made new." – Ursula K LeGuin, American author

You cannot ignore love of family; like bread, it will go stale.

THE GENOS, PART TWO

The Geno family is an example of a business that survived when they separated the personal from the business. What they had lost was family trust. Trust is difficult when the family doesn't have the time to really know one another. While the business survived, the family relationships have not.

When Mr. Geno passes away, what will happen to his business and the family relationships? Family members who have had little contact with one another, personally or in business, will then become partners.

My prediction is that, if the company is to survive, the family relationships must dramatically improve. Without the FAMILY FIRST commitment, will they really care about the success of each family member or will they just be out to get what they can? It will be interesting! But maybe not pleasant.

Other FAMILY FIRST Thoughts

Families who are in business together naturally have more opportunities for conflict. Each family member must decide what comes first in their family and business relationship. Business at all cost? *My* success at all cost? Or the realization that the success of the family in business offers much more opportunity for mutual and individual success?

Making a choice to put FAMILY FIRST begins with family success being placed above self-interest. FAMILY FIRST means each family member taking on the responsibility for assisting the others to be as successful as they can possibly be. FAMILY FIRST means family members choosing to be there for one another in business as well as their personal lives, even when another may not have always supported them.

KWAISERISM

You will know that you place FAMILY FIRST when you care about your family members' happiness and success more than you do your own. True family love can overcome anything.

FAMILY FIRST is love of family in the good times and bad, when it is easy and when it is difficult. FAMILY FIRST means not allowing family to do whatever they want to do; not enabling the poor behavior of one family member, one who is self-serving at the cost of family reputation or success.

FAMILY FIRST means being honest and supportive of every family member, even the one who may have to be separated from the business because of his or her choice to not live and practice the FAMILY FIRST values. Separation is difficult and should only come after lovingly, directly, addressing the issues and possible resolutions, then giving the individual the chance to make the choice of FAMILY FIRST. If that's not possible, the family needs to commit to support this individual in whatever he or she wishes to do that is legal and does not infringe on the reputation of the family or family business.

FAMILY FIRST is a real choice for a family working and supporting each other for mutual success. FAMILY FIRST means love is freely offered and accepted, practicing trust and respect, but also being truthful and honest with those who are not keeping commitments to the family and the business. It is placing family before self.

FAMILY FIRST should be discussed, understood and practiced in all families and all family businesses. More open, trusting, adult conversations will result in better understanding, trust and respect for one another.

Without FAMILY FIRST, without open, honest communication, or objective advisers, or rules, or commitment, or the proper preparation, the family and business will always suffer. You can have the best organizational chart, a great financial plan and a lot of legal documents—and still you will not survive as a successful family business. You will become another one of those two-thirds of family businesses that fail before the end of the second generation.

Have you discussed the priority of FAMILY FIRST with your family? Maybe that conversation should take place—SOON.

Other Thoughts on Family Love and Family Business

Family businesses are being attacked on several fronts. While many view competition, market conditions and the economy as major causes of failure, they are looking in the wrong places.

Lack of trust, not valuing one another's opinion, a "me first" mentality, greed and fear are the real causes of most family business failures. Each of these can be directly related to a family members' attitude toward family love.

Family love is more than just saying "I love my family." Family love means that each family member is motivated by the best interest of the family and the business. Each needs to place the family before self and the family business before their individual personal desires.

KWAISERISM

Demonstrative love of the family is FAMILY FIRST in action.

Family love means admitting mistakes and committing to not making them again, and forgiving and trusting in the motives of each family member until proven differently. Family love means identifying family members who cannot buy in to the FAMILY FIRST philosophy, and supporting these individuals by helping them find whatever they may be successful doing.

Competition, market conditions and the economy are certainly areas to consider when creating your strategic business plan and certainly can be major threats to your business. But the most serious attack on your business can come from within. The lack of real family love and respect is the cause of most family business failures.

The whole concept of family love must be discussed, understood and put into practice by every family member in the business. This fosters individual respect, better, more timely decisions and business growth. The best strategic plans cannot be completed without all the family members involved on the same page, working toward a common goal.

When your business is being attacked, you need to understand the competition, market conditions and the economy. But, as a family business, make sure you are looking in the right places. Begin with every family member committing to the real meaning of family love in your business. Your success or failure will depend upon it.

Another example of choosing the wrong priorities.

THE GOODSELLS

The Dysfunctional

Bill and Susan Goodsell and their eldest daughter Josey, were instrumental in the success of the business. When the time came for the other adult children, Chuck and Ed, to enter the business, Josey protested, saying, "There just is no place for them at the present time." Josey's protest was not made because of the financial condition of the business; she felt her siblings coming into the business might seem unfair to other employees and affect the year-end bonuses of the key personnel. FAMILY FIRST took a back seat to bonuses and what others may think.

The advisor suggested that the salaries and expenses of Chuck and Ed be tracked under the appropriate departments but their expenses would not affect any bonuses or incentives for the rest of the fiscal year. While Josey agreed to this arrangement she still protested her brothers coming into the business. She has threatened to quit if they do.

The Goodsells are stuck on this situation as they are in effect being held hostage by Josie. Currently discussions and ideas to resolve these issues are continuing, with a reluctant Josie. Unfortunately, there is a definite conflict between FAMILY FIRST and "me first" thinking. This may truly be the end of the story for this family and business.

Like Josey, some family members are willing to forfeit their relationships with each other to keep the business intact. There are many consultants who profess a "save the company at any cost" philosophy that can direct families away from each other.

Family and business priorities must be discussed early in the succession planning process. FAMILY FIRST versus business first can easily bring up emotions that will change family priorities; this must be addressed. This

KWAISERISM

Communication is a key ingredient to successful family relationships.

difference can also cause everyone to be thinking about succession issues, but afraid to bring them out into the open. They may be unsure what the answers will be, so to avoid conflict they make it an unspeakable. If there are marked differences in priorities, a different direction for estate planning and a new structure to ensure the continuation of the business will have to be devised. Selling the business to keep the family intact may become a viable option.

All family members need to take FAMILY FIRST seriously. If decisions concerning the business start to tear apart family relationships, pit parents against adult children, adult children against each other, and even parents against each other by siding with different adult children, the question must be asked, "Is the money worth it?" If a person is persistent enough, another job can be found; another family cannot. People get divorced, lose their health and wealth, and a close family can still be supportive.

Unfortunately, ego, greed, jealously, envy, and favoritism enter into the hearts of some family members and their only focus becomes "my cut" of the business. A spouse may begin to push their mate to "get their fair share" from the business and the estate. This often happens because the spouse has never been kept up-to-date on how decisions have been made or what agreements the siblings have worked out.

The purpose of the annual family meeting discussed previously is to share information about how the company is run with those not involved in the day-to-day operations. While these meetings are not designed to solve the top priority problems, they will promote understanding of the business and open communication among the whole family. This communication meeting will help stress that everyone is important to the success of the business.

Additionally, the FAMILY FIRST belief that all are important to the business is reinforced. When those who are not active in the business have a better understanding and know that family is first, attitudes toward to the business by all improve.

CHAPTER 10

ENLIGHTEN WITH PERSONAL EXPERIENCES

As kids, most of us love to hear stories. Whether they were real, read out of a book, or just made up as they were being told. Bed-time books and story breaks during the day were times that we looked forward to, along with hearing stories from our parents or grandparents. When most kids are asking to help with what is going on with the business, they see this as a privilege and not as work at all. With these facts in mind, we can see why it is important to not only share stories about the business when the children are young, but also to get them involved. Give them responsibility and accountability in the business, no matter how small it may seem.

THE BLANCHARDS

Steve Blanchard started his software business right out of college. He spent many long hours building the business and, when he married Barbara, she played an active role in the administration of the business.

The business grew, and is still growing, including the purchase of their own office building. Their family is also growing as Steve and Barb now have three children: Denise, 13; Alex, 11; and Beth, 6.

All three have a role in the business. From filing of invoices by Denise, fixing things in the building once a week with his Dad and the maintenance people for Alex, and shredding papers for Beth. All three are gaining an appreciation for work and are beginning to realize no matter what the task, each person in the company contributes to the overall success of the company when they all do their best.

Each of the children is told stories of why their jobs are so important—stories about overflowing papers, lost invoices, and burned out lights that keep people from doing their job as effectively as they could. Even for Beth, the stories of what can happen if scrap paper and invoices are not taken care of in a proper, timely fashion. When the family comes together for their family business meeting, the children discuss their roles and what they have learned, and then share ways to improve them. They learn accountability, responsibility and how their tasks can have a major impact on others in the company. They learn to openly discuss each job and how each benefits the company. They talk openly without malice about how each area may be improved. All these are lessons that will be carried, in a positive way, into adulthood. All are experiences that will help each of the children to compete and bring benefit to any job and any company they may work for.

Stay tuned for the rest of the story.

When all members of the business share their experiences with each other, tell war stories, and give examples of their own successes and failures, this enables each family member to expand their own knowledge of the company.

The Dysfunctional

When this type of communication and participation does not take place, these issues can become unspeakables. This takes place because no one wants to share their part of the business world—some call this job security—or maybe embarrass one another, or admit when their own failure has occurred. Not sharing stories about their jobs is a tremendous waste of many meaningful learning experiences!

The Extraordinary

Sharing experiences can save people from making wrong decisions a second or third time, saving the company money and customers. Doing the right thing for the benefit of the company adds to the success of everyone in the company, emphasizing the need to always set the example by your attitude, words, and actions. More on this will be shared in Chapter 11.

Time should be scheduled to share experiences and stories at regular, scheduled family business meetings. The family can learn from each other if each takes the time to listen. Listen to parents, siblings and other key company employees. The more the family communicates, the better they know one another, the more trust will build. The business will not only become successful but will become a place the family wants to go to be close to their family. This will enable each family member to re-experience the feelings of assisting in the family business when they were younger.

THE BLANCHARDS, PART TWO

Fifteen years have passed for the Blanchards. Steve and Barb still share experiences, not only with their family but with the employees as well. Key members meet each week, share stories, ask for assistance and are open to the suggestions of others. They all know that their success hangs upon each member of the company being successful.

Denise and Alex had decided to stay with the business as their future. Denise received her Master's Degree in Information Technology and has a BS in Business Administration. Alex also has a degree in Business Administration and is working on his Masters in Organizational Leadership. Beth is a senior in college with a double major in accounting and business administration.

Denise, as the Chief Informational Officer, heads up the research and development of original programs and systems to be added to the company services and product line. Alex is Chief Organizational Officer, ensuring the right people are in the right positions and developing, along with other key employees, the strategic direction for the company. Alex also directs which people and assets are to be allocated to what area of the company based upon the approved strategic direction.

In addition to choosing areas of study that are a best fit for them and the company, Denise and Alex are ready for their positions because of the on-going input of stories and experiences from their parents and others in the company. Once Beth graduates she will work for the company's CFO, gain experience, and be groomed for that position when the current CFO retires in five years.

Tips On Telling Stories

Telling stories, offering examples to follow, and having others participate are positive traits of successful families in business. One tip is for every member of the family business to become teachers to one another; this is also one of the most difficult traits to master.

Today we find the workforce, more than ever before, responds negatively to most pure directive instruction. They interpret this style as demeaning and view it as being a corrective action instead of instruction. In the past, directive instruction was a call to action for most workers to wake up and get on track. A call to work harder. Now we find such instruction has just the opposite effect.

Most leaders used to give orders but rarely give reasons for why a particular task had to be completed. Unfortunately, most still do. Rarely do leaders view each interaction with their employees as an opportunity to teach; to tell a story of the importance of what needs to be done and the positive impact it can have on all involved.

KWAISERISM

Know that you are teaching others whether you want to or not!

Yes, not all instruction can come with the full story behind it but, in reality, most can be explained better. Taking the time to explain our reasoning, or the effect of decisions, to tell the story behind the decisions, will enable others to buy in and support what is being done.

Teaching is hard. Rarely do we take the time to teach our employees about decision making and big picture impact. This new generation of employees, including our children who hopefully will be our successors, have a very strong need to know, to feel as though they are a part of the decision even if it was made in advance. If decisions are presented and discussed before implementation, understanding takes place and the buy-in to the decision is greater.

This teaching, including telling the story of how the decision was made, also helps employees understand the steps to decision-making in the company. This understanding will allow for faster decisions in all areas of the company as everyone understands the decision-making process and how it works. Storytelling teaching helps employees use the solutions identified in the story to find innovative solutions to other problems.

Dictatorship stresses everyone. Teaching brings long-term, innovative results to future problems. Only when teaching is not accepted do pure directives have to be given. Even when this does happen, explaining why this needs to be done in a certain way, and the affect it has on the company and the employees, becomes a teaching story.

Yes, taking on the role of a teacher and a storyteller will stress you out initially, and will take more time than you want to give, initially. But in the long run, the time lost on repeated mistakes will eventually diminish; your people will have a greater appreciation for their job. They will become more productive.

When we were kids we used to love having our parents and others tell us stories. A story is nothing more than the telling of events and usually impacts others either for good or bad.

So not every story has to be a book. They just have to have a beginning, a middle, and an end which includes a conclusion showing how it affected the people in the story.

So, let's all become kids again. Let's tell the stories behind our decisions and listen to the stories of those we work with for input, suggestions and innovative ideas. When we do, succession will be smoother, employees will be happier, and innovation will become a normal occurrence.

Other Thoughts on Stories and Feedback

For companies to grow, you need to get open feedback from as many of your employees as possible. Yep, some will tell you stories that will be bogus, but most will be very useful *if* you are willing to listen.

A friend shared with me an article by J.W Marriott, Jr., including advice he was given by President Dwight Eisenhower about managing people:

"Before you give your advice and recommendations ask the question, 'What do you think we should do?'

I have been a strong advocate of this advice, but I also believe in taking this one step further. We should also ask "Why do you think we should do this?" and wait to hear their story. Why should this be done? How should this be done? What impact will this have on the people involved?

When you discover the full story behind the suggestions they offer, the more you understand their thought processes and the more you get to know them. The more you know your employees, the better the opportunity for you to be able to trust their judgment and decisions. When this trust becomes practice, your company will grow much quicker as decisions by others becomes more trusted and timely. Better, faster decisions usually

KWAISERISM

Instructions, directives, suggestions and opinions are only stories that are needed to explain the situation.

What needs to be done, why it needs to be done and the impact it has on the characters— encourage these stories.

save money and time. Your company becomes more successful by your personal trust of the stories of your people.

Another side benefit is that your personal stress level actually goes down when your people are making the decisions you hired them to do. This is usually a difficult step for many entrepreneurs because they will no longer be micro-managing; they view this as a loss of control and power. They have this view even when passing the business onto their next generation.

In reality, when you ask questions and listen to their answers as stories, you will better understand someone's thinking processes. These question and discussion sessions are great opportunities for you to teach others to make decisions like you do. How fast would your company grow, how well could you take care of your family and employees if you had five people who could make decisions like you? You cannot grow your company by yourself. Tell and listen to stories and you will develop others to be able to make decisions the same way you do.

CHAPTER 11

SET AN **EXAMPLE**

An example of effective family business leaders
Extraordinary from the start!

THE SAMPSONS

Pat and Danna Sampson began their real-estate company just after they married. They had met in real-estate school and their relationship grew to love, life and business partnership.

They have two sons, Pat Jr. and Don. Both entered the business after college and helped their Mom and Dad grow it. The business now has 16 agents and four support people in two offices. Pat Sr. and Danna coached their sons in all aspects of the business. They had them evaluated on how they were progressing by an impartial third party who they respected. Their sons took to the business quickly and were soon proficient enough to begin to coach others.

Pat Sr. and Danna are respected as the leaders of the company and are viewed as equal partners. Pat Jr. and Don both have identified roles with accountability, responsibility and authority known by all employees. Both Pat Sr. and Danna mentor their sons to take over the day-to-day operations of the business, using information from the impartial third party.

The Extraordinary

Pat and Danna led by example. They had regular communication meetings with all the employees, keeping them updated on sales and growth, as well as actively listening to the input and ideas of their people. No subjects were off limits and each open topic was assigned, researched and voted upon. Every meeting had an agenda with input from the participants; minutes were taken and distributed; and everyone knew what they were accountable and responsible for and what day-to-day decisions they were expected to make. They also knew that they could get help and support from anyone in the company.

Innovation was encouraged, no ideas were discounted and each new accomplishment was rewarded and celebrated. Each employee understood the sense of urgency in answering client's questions and concerns, and all went out of their way to make the buying experience as painless as possible.

The family enabled all employees to feel as though they were a real part of the business family, keeping them informed, having them involved in decisions that affect them, listening to what they say, looking at mistakes as ways to improve, and treating them with respect. That is the reason why most of their employees have been at the company for 10 years or more.

Pat, Danna and their sons set the example every day for what it means to be effective leaders. When they had disagreements, the employees never knew it. They placed family and their employees before the business and the business continued to grow because of it.

Today, Sampson Real Estate has five offices around the state. Pat Jr. and Don are now running the day-to-day operations and have

> kept their parents' management style intact. Pat Sr. and Danna are now co-chairpersons of the Board of Directors and continue to act as advisors to their sons. They also visit each location on a regular basis as goodwill ambassadors for their sons. The business continues to grow with innovation, creativity and long-term, loyal employees. Everything we want a family business to have. They just aren't "normal."

Other Thoughts on Leadership and Example in a Family Business

Being part of a family business is not always easy. Children who think that mom and dad are out of touch with today's business ideas, and parents who believe their children, even after 20 years, are still not ready to take over, can cause conflict and family dissention. Siblings who believe they are short-changed when dad and mom select the other one to be the successor, create more problems with family relationships. Dealing with banks and vendors, as well as customers who don't pay on time is not easy. Some employees don't seem to care, have no loyalty and will leave for an extra dime.

Hiring and firing is not easy either. Sorting through hundreds of resumes to find three people, and then have only one of them show up for work is part of leadership frustration!

Firing is often the most difficult for most leaders in family businesses. Even when they know that an employee is not really a fit for the position, many leaders procrastinate when making the firing decision. This delay causes the loss of good, productive individuals who just don't believe things will get better, a lowering of morale, and an overall lack of trust in the company leaders.

Nobody said running a business would be easy. Leaders in a family businesses must take responsibility and set the example for the care and morale of all their people, family and non-family members alike. Each leader must make sure that all their managers are properly handling all issues and leading by example. Of course, it isn't easy, but, as a friend of mine recently commented, "Don't complain, it's what you signed up for."

Thoughts on the Example of Servant Leadership

Over the years, a lot has been written about Servant Leadership. Three books I recommend are *Servant Leadership* by Robert Greenleaf, *The Servant Leader* by James Autry, and *Laws of Leadership* by John Maxwell. Setting the example is at the core of the Servant Leadership philosophy, encouraging leaders to consciously serve the people who work for them.

KWAISERISM

If leadership and entrepreneurship were easy, everyone would be doing it!

At first blush this concept appears faulty and has been misinterpreted to mean leaders should give their employees everything they want. Because of this misconception, many leaders have not embraced this philosophy. The question still in several minds is: "How can a leader function properly if he is to serve his employees?"

To begin to understand the Servant Leadership concept, business owners must realize two important truths. First, no one person can make a company successful. Other people must be involved. Second, when a leader serves his or her people by ensuring they have the right training, the right tools and equipment, and the authority to do their jobs, they will have a feeling of security that they are contributing to the success of the company. This will make them more productive and the company more profitable.

Servant Leadership does not mean caving into employees, giving them whatever they want. In fact, it's the opposite. Servant Leadership means a management style that is firm and fair. Treating people in a manner and in a voice that is understood and consistent. Treating them like human beings and not just tools to get a job done. Caring for employees' welfare as individuals as well as members of your company team.

Will some people try to take advantage of you? Yes! It happens every day. But, instead of turning the leader sour on his employees, he should realize that over 80+% of them are trying to do the right thing day in and day out. These are the people who should be served.

You cannot serve people who don't want the company to succeed; they are a detriment to everyone. Servant Leaders must let go of those who do not want to succeed by using the Servant Leadership Philosophy.

Servant Leadership is not for the faint of heart. Dedication and a commitment to excellence means accepting nothing less. Your loyalty to those who are willing to follow your example by serving others inside and outside the company pays off.

Servant Leadership is needed today more than ever with our varied and diverse workforce of changing loyalties. Today's workforce wants and needs more interaction with the company leaders. The strategies of Servant Leadership, when properly understood, can enable leaders to fill that need plus grow future leaders. Check out the resources listed at the end of this book, and take a look at how to implement Servant Leadership in your company.

More on Leadership and Teaching by Example

"After demonstration of commitment and self-less attitude toward family and business, what traits should I be teaching the next generation?"

This question is brought to us often. The most difficult separations to identify for both the senior and next generation are the differences between leadership and management. Our definition of a manager is one who controls the behavior of employees, directing them to successful accomplishment of tasks. Our definition of a leader is one who explains a vision of a desired future, influencing others to cooperate in attaining that goal, not for selfish gain, but for the success of all involved.

Many members of the senior generation coach on management but seldom on leadership. They stress tasks instead of the direction of the company. Many of the next generation want to go straight to leadership without understanding the methods of a manager or the meaning of true leadership. They feel they can direct others and then sit back while others get the job done.

KWAISERISM

Teach more than just tasks.

Teach what it means to have the heart of a leader.

In most family businesses, the next generation need to learn both management and leadership. They must be hands-on managers, willing to do what it takes to help the company be successful. They must be selfless visionaries, concerned about the success of each family member and every employee. They must be example setters and follow the lead of the examples of the rest of the family.

Watch how the next generation manages themselves. Help them to understand the roles they are about to take on. When observing and evaluating, ask questions such as:

1. Do they make effective use of their time?
2. Do they show up on time and follow through the way they should?
3. Do they listen to the input of others and ask for help when making decisions?
4. Are they constant learners?
5. Do they strive to be the best they can be in their industry?

KWAISERISM

Perceptions are not always reality. Listen and learn.

Make a list of questions, including the examples given, and review these with your potential successors. Let them know this is part of the criteria that they will be evaluated on. Inform them that, without practicing and demonstrating the traits of management and leadership, they will most likely join the two-thirds of family businesses that don't make it through to the second generation. If they understand, all you have worked so hard to pass on will survive as a strong, lasting legacy.

Most leaders are good at perception, the "gut" insight or intuition they use to make decisions and judgments. How many times have we allowed our first impressions make the decisions for us? Probably more than you want to admit to!

While we use our perceptions as a guide to making business decisions, is this the right trait to use when judging people? We often size up others by how they look and come to conclusions without ever speaking to the individual.

As leaders, are we obligated to have a more open mind about our employees? We probably should, yet there are times when we all fall short in this area. Have you ever made a judgment about another person when you met them for the first time? Or without ever meeting them? Have you ever allowed your first impression to influence your judgment, but after getting to know the individual you found that you were wrong? We have all done it.

Our first impressions determine our perceptions of others. As leaders, we must guard against judging on first impressions and allow individuals to show us who they are by their words and actions.

Recently I met a fellow who looked as though he had just come from living on the street, but someone had put him in a suit and tie. I had already made up my mind that this meeting was going to be a real bust. Then we started talking. He was articulate, smart and experienced, and as we began to discuss several issues I no longer saw a "bum in a suit." I saw a professional who looked different than what I expected. This really brought home to me (yes, I too need reminding occasionally) that first impressions can be wrong. We need to spend a little more time getting to know others *before* we allow our initial perceptions to take over our judgment.

Think about your own company. Are there people in your company who you have pegged with some identification and yet you have not really spent time with them? Effective leaders must take the time to get to know their employees. People often open up, offer more suggestions, and are more innovative when they know that their leaders care for them and value their opinions. If the leaders don't, they will be missing an opportunity to promote or gain valuable insight from employees who work in the system and maybe know the company better than most of those in management.

KWAISERISM

Great leaders, great people are known for the examples they set.

Take the time to really get to know your employees and let them know you. Rotating a breakfast or lunch with them is a great way to do this. In larger companies, get your key managers involved in this effort and have them feedback their findings.

More employees will see that there is true Servant Leadership and caring for the input of all employees. In many ways, you can change incorrect perceptions that you and your management team have. Who knows, you may even correct the employees' perceptions of management!

Set the Example by Your Attitude, Words and Actions

Family members must show their commitment to one another by their actions. They need to lead by example so other family members can follow.

Whether the children will live out the example in a positive or negative way is affected dramatically by the person whose example was observed

KWAISERISM

(stolen from somewhere but oft quoted by my wife):

"Patience is a virtue. Seek it if you can.

Often found in women— never in a man."

I am not sure I believe this, but I am practicing patience!

and how it was interpreted. Usually the parents are the first to be observed, then the siblings.

Attitude toward the business, positive outlook, and positive interactions are communicated by example. Helping the children and allowing them to help each other understand the difference between entitlement and responsibility can eliminate much of the jealousy that can grow when one thinks another has received more than their share from dad and mom.

"What's in it for me?" feelings can be especially damaging in family businesses. A feeling of entitlement has a strong relationship to how much one feels loved in the family. If a specific child is perceived to get more from the estate of the parents or from the business in the form of position, ownership, salary, or perks, other family members may believe they are not favored; that they are less loved; that they were not treated fairly and equally. This perception can destroy relationships and the business may have to be sold to resolve a misunderstood fairness issue.

Properly addressing the C.H.A.L.L.E.N.G.E.S. of family businesses must start with the example set by the parents, passed on to the children, and then practiced by them. Parents must place emphasis on the responsibility for open, honest communication with each member of the family.

Just imagine how successful every family and every business would be if everyone involved was totally unselfish, put others in the family first, always set a positive example for others to follow, helped others to be the best they could be, and then took joy in the success others achieved.

The C.H.A.L.L.E.N.G.E.S. of family business can be most successfully addressed by properly stirring the pot of conflict and emotion, addressing the issues, forgiving, loving, and setting the example.

Leadership and the Example of Patience

Members of family businesses are different from one another. So why do some want others to think and act exactly like they do? Ego and emotion get in the way and patience is missing. This can lead to big disagreements and even shouting matches.

Patience in a family business is the art of really listening to what another says and not discounting it. Patience means not being so locked into what you want to get across that you do not hear the feelings, thoughts or opinions of others. Not only your ideas and thoughts matter. Patience means taking the time to really hear what others say. Too many times we discount others' ideas or feelings because of our impatience.

Patience means keeping emotional control even when under strain, when others are pushing your buttons to try to make you act or react in a certain way. Wikipedia says that patience is a "state of endurance under difficult circumstances."

Many members of family businesses (and many families) rarely think about patience as a virtue or value they should be practicing. Maybe you should re-evaluate your commitment to patience. Do not interrupt others' conversations; listen with an open mind to the ideas of others, to really hear what is important to other family members and be there for them. What might be an annoyance to you can be important to another family member.

Through patience we will be able to show respect for the feelings of other family members. We may not agree with their feelings, but we need to acknowledge those feelings. Because of our love for them we need to practice the virtue of patience to show them how much we do care. Patience is a *must* for every business and every family.

CHAPTER 12

FAMILY AND FEELINGS
FROM A WOMAN'S PERSPECTIVE

by Ann Marie Kwaiser

Take the feelings of family seriously

Feelings of your family members, whether you think they are warranted or not, can't be denied. Feelings, whether of being happy or hurt, of being in love or angry, in need of forgiveness or comfort, whatever they are or consist of, must be respected. They are very real to those expressing them. Maybe you have said this yourself, and I am sure that you have had other people say this to you: "Don't feel that way," or "You shouldn't feel that way." No one should ever downplay anyone's feelings.

As a woman, wife, mother and business partner, I have learned that feelings, no matter whose, must be respected. Feelings spring from emotion. Emotions can be real or perceived, but they are real to the individual experiencing them.

Try as you may, changing the way a person feels is difficult if not impossible. We need to accept feelings for what they are—the attitudes and beliefs that have been formed by the person sharing them. All people have a right to their feelings, and we need to show enough respect to listen, to make our best effort to take seriously the feelings of those we love.

The other day Jim and I were traveling between appointments and we began talking as we usually do—imagine that after 48 years of marriage we still share with one another and express our honest feelings to one another. We know the other will listen and give our beliefs, our feelings, the respect they deserve just because we love one another.

During this conversation, we were discussing if changing feelings was possible. Jim asked if I thought a person could really change his or her feelings. After tossing a few thoughts back and forth, we both agreed that, for a person to really change how they feel about something, they first must have an inner mind-set change. This can only happen if they have a real change of heart, which takes a conscious effort, an open mind, and independent research.

Feelings are confusing at times. With some people, you may feel as though you have known them forever. With others, no matter how long you have known them you never get the feeling you will ever be close. Sharing feelings with clients, friends and even acquaintances can even be easier than sharing them with family. Sad but true. Too often our family places several restrictions on us and how we should feel.

I had a meeting with a wife of a CEO not long ago. During our luncheon, I asked her how she felt about a delicate situation in the company. She looked at me with tears in her eyes and allowed the outpouring of the feelings that had been withheld for so long.

The most amazing part of this conversation was her statement, "I feel so much better having shared this with you. I was able to share with you what I could never say to my husband or family."

Amazed, I asked her why she could not share this with her family. She stated that I had never discounted or downplayed her feelings. I was not judgmental. I never told her that her feelings were wrong or that she should feel one way or another.

Our relationship began to grow out of the trust that we could share our feelings openly with one another, whether we agreed or not, because we never ridiculed or discounted each other's feelings.

Once Jim and I arrived home after our client travels we went about our work for the afternoon. The conversation we had about feelings continued to enter my thoughts and I could not shake them. I was thinking about how relationships are made or lost because of one person's attitude toward another individual's feelings. I wrote down some thoughts about family and feelings. Then I set this list aside and did not think about it for a while.

One day Jim asked if I would write a chapter for the book he was working on. He wanted to have a chapter on something concerning families in business from a women's perspective. At first, I felt that I could never come up with a topic that would fit. Then, I thought of my list of family and feelings, and I said I would give it a shot.

I was glad he wanted my input and said that it was important. Then again, he has always asked for my input, my feelings, about his thoughts, as well as personal and business issues.

Respect for one another's feelings cannot be lost in a family business. Isn't that what strong relationships are built around—respect? I am the chief advisor in his life and he is the chief advisor in mine.

A while ago I read a story about a retired couple who were very successful. Robert was a retired banker and Marie was a supportive wife, who excelled at her role as wife of a bank president. Robert and Marie, now that they had the time, decided to take a trip back to their home state of West Virginia, to see friends and relatives. After making the decision to take the back roads for a leisurely drive, they packed their new Cadillac and headed out.

The scenery was as beautiful as the day. They decided to stop and get some refreshments as well as fill the gas tank, so they stopped at an old gas station. Robert went inside to get some bottled water. As he headed in, a man about his age, but with greasy overalls and gritty hands, came out of the garage. Robert asked him to fill it up. The greasy man just nodded and headed for the car. Inside the store, Robert found a disheveled woman behind the counter who waited on him.

When Robert came out of the store he saw Marie standing outside the car, talking and laughing with the greasy station attendant. She had her hand on his arm as they talked to each other. When Robert walked up, Marie introduced him to the attendant. His name was Mark and they had gone to school together. They also had dated a few times.

As Robert and Marie were leaving, she gave Mark a hug and Robert courteously shook his hand. After they pulled away from the station, Robert turned to Marie and said, "Lucky you didn't marry him. You would have ended up behind the counter selling water!"

"No, my love," Marie said, "If I had married him, he would have been the banker and you would have been pumping gas!"

Always remember who your chief advisors really are—the people closest to you, who have your best interest at heart, and who will always, in an honest way, express their feelings to you. Do not ignore or discount the feelings of those who love you. They could make the difference in how your life plays out.

Consideration and respect should be given to all the feelings of others, especially family. What seems a petty feeling to you may be a huge problem for the other individual and visa-versa! If you both really care for one another, all your feelings are important to those you love and theirs become important to you.

I will end with the following story that was sent to me by a friend, as an example of unconditional love and the importance of understanding others' feelings. This is a lesson for all of us to live and to pass on to future generations.

Burned Biscuits

A friend of mine told me the following story—appropriate when we discuss feelings. I hope that it means as much to you as it does to me.

When I was a kid, my Mom liked to make breakfast food for dinner every now and then. One night she had made breakfast after a long, hard day at work. On that evening so long ago, my Mom placed a plate of eggs, sausage and extremely burned biscuits in front of my Dad. I waited to see if anyone noticed! Yet all my Dad did was reach for his biscuit, smile at my Mom, and ask me how my day was at school. I don't remember what I told him that night, but I do remember watching him smear butter and jelly on that biscuit and eat every bite!

When I got up from the table that evening, I heard my Mom apologize to my Dad for burning the biscuits. I'll never forget what he said: "Honey, I love burned biscuits."

Later that night, I went to kiss Daddy good night and asked him if he really liked his biscuits burned. He wrapped me in his arms and said, "Your Momma put in a hard day at work today and she's real tired. And besides—a little burned biscuit never hurt anyone!"

Life is full of imperfect things and imperfect people. I'm not the best at hardly anything, and I forget birthdays and anniversaries just like everyone else. But what I've learned over the years is that learning to accept each other's faults and feelings—and choosing to celebrate each other's differences—are the most important keys to creating a healthy, growing, and lasting relationship.

KWAISERISM

"Without feelings, there is no love."

That's my prayer for you today. I pray you will learn to take the good, the bad, and the ugly parts of your life and lay them at the feet of God. Because in the end, He's the only One who will be able to give you a relationship where a burnt biscuit isn't a deal-breaker! Understanding is the basis of any relationship, husband-wife, parent-child or friendship!

Don't put the key to your happiness in someone else's pocket. Keep it in your own. "So please pass me a biscuit, and yes, the burned one will do just fine."

Please pass this story along to someone who has enriched your life. Be kinder than necessary because everyone you meet is fighting some kind of battle.

Life without God is like an unsharpened pencil—it has no point.

ANN MARIE'S
Other Thoughts on Feelings

Family love has to carry over into the business. There has to be a commitment to place family before business. Making a choice of FAMILY FIRST begins with members placing family success above self-interest. As described in the first chapter, FAMILY FIRST has each family member taking on the responsibility for assisting other family members to be as successful as they can possibly be.

The key principles of FAMILY FIRST deserve repeating. Family members need to choose to be there for one another in the business as well as their personal lives, even for someone who may not have always supported them.

FAMILY FIRST is love of family in the good times and bad, when it is easy and when it is hard. FAMILY FIRST is not allowing family to do whatever they want to do, not enabling the poor behavior of a family member, not allowing them to be self-serving at the cost of family reputation or success.

FAMILY FIRST means being honest and supportive of every family member, even those who may have to be separated from the business because of their choice to not live and practice FAMILY FIRST values. Separation is difficult and should only come after lovingly, directly addressing the issues, searching for resolutions, and giving the individual a chance to choose FAMILY FIRST. If they don't make this choice, the family must commit to support this individual in whatever they wish to do that is legal and does not infringe on the reputation of the family or business.

FAMILY FIRST means a family choosing to work and support one another for mutual success. Love must be freely offered and accepted. In addition to practicing trust and respect, FAMILY FIRST means being truthful and honest with family members who are not keeping commitments to the family and business.

FAMILY FIRST is a concept that should be discussed, understood and practiced in all families and family businesses. This will lead to more open, trusting, adult conversations resulting in better understanding, trust and respect for one another This bears repetition until it becomes second nature to your business.

Have you discussed true FAMILY FIRST with your family? Maybe now is time for that conversation to take place.

CHAPTER 13

AN **EXTRAORDINARY** FAMILY IN BUSINESS

Love = Faith, Family, Future

Most family businesses do describe themselves as "normal" because they are dysfunctional. They really believe that a dysfunctional family is the way most families in business are naturally. That is just the nature of a family working together in business.

We do not believe that has to be "normal." The preceding chapters have given you real-life examples of how several families have transformed from the "dysfunctional normal," to the no longer "normal" family business; they have become "extra-ordinary" in their relationships with one another and in their unified focus for all to be successful. We have also described families in business who refused or were unable to make the commitment to FAMILY FIRST. Because of this inability, these families remained dysfunctional, with strained interpersonal relationships and, as a result, face major challenges trying to keep the company afloat.

This chapter highlights the Burgs family as an example of the extraordinary family and business. Yes, they have many of the same problems of other families. They disagree with one another; they don't always see eye to eye; they may argue about how to get a certain task or job done. All families have some conflict. What separates the "normal dysfunctional" from the "above normal extraordinary" is how those conflicts are handled.

THE BURGS

The Burgs are totally on the same page when it comes to the vision and culture of the family and the business. There is no lack of trust in one another. They all realize that each person is looking out for the best interest of the family and the company.

There is open, honest communication. They schedule uninterrupted time for the family to plan, discuss, reach agreements and just plain talk with one another.

They know their relationships are based on family love and that none of them would intentionally hurt one another. They stick together and find the solutions that are right for their family and the business. The Burgs believe in FAMILY FIRST and that the success of the family is more important than individual success. They are "extra-ordinary."

Stan and Nena Burgs dated through college, got married and started a family. Stan founded a business providing equipment and supplies to the oil drilling industry. His motivation was to feed his family and work on his own terms. Nena soon joined the company, handling administration and human resource duties. Stan and Nina were not looking to build a generational business. They were looking to make a living.

Stan and Nena have three children. Joanna came along first, then Vernon and finally Anthony. The kids are close, with mutual respect and trust for one another and for their parents. The parents share a strong faith and passed that on to their children. Their faith is a guide for their relationships with one another and others and defines their personal and business values. Their faith is the roadmap for how they make decisions and the foundation for their future.

Stan and Nena work hard at growing the business. In the beginning their life was full of the day-to-day activity of working and raising their children. They determined early on that growth of a profitable business was the best way to put food on the table and care for their children. They also decided to be honest in their business dealings, pay their bills on time, and protect their employees as best as they could.

When the children were small, like most entrepreneurs, Stan and Nena did not even consider the possibility of having any of them come into the business as a career. In fact, they encouraged them to work elsewhere and did not discuss succession with their children.

The kids were assigned a variety of tasks in the business when they were small, and, as they grew, they worked there summers and holidays. To them, being children of the owners meant doing any job asked, without complaint, working harder than anyone else, and thereby earning the respect of others in the company. When they were in high school, none of the children seriously considered the family business as a career. It was just what Mom and Dad did.

In addition to being the founder and owner, Stan always was one of the workers in the business. He drove the truck, delivered the product, fixed the machinery and did every job in the company at some time. He began to realize that, to expand the business and increase his income for a growing family, he would have to learn how to be more involved working *on* the business.

This meant that he would have to find qualified people to handle more of the tasks he was currently doing. To plan better, to use the financials for decision-making, and to reorganize the company for growth, became his priorities. Management succession was at the top of his priority list. Stan and Nena prayed on the decision and then hired us to assist with succession planning and organizational development.

The first step centered around the growth of the company and ensuring the right people were in the right positions. With Stan and Nena, we began to review and evaluate all the key players in the business. This showed that some of these were at the top end of their experience and knowledge, so they no longer had the expertise to lead in growing the business. Each position and individual was re-evaluated based on what was going to be needed for the future, not what the company had accomplished up to this point.

Many of these individuals were given the opportunity to move into a position where they could continue to grow with the company. It became evident that some of their employees would not accept the change and would eventually have to leave the company. We cautioned Stan and Nena that one of these people would, more than likely, be the one that the Burgs would think to be the least likely. Stan and Nena prepared for that possibility and were not shocked when their key employee resigned a few weeks later. Others stepped up to the plate and the company continued to prosper.

A board of advisors was created with Stan, Nena, their children and the two consultants. Although the children were still in high school, the non-family board members determined that they were mature enough to begin to experience the company from an executive point of view. Their on-going experiences in the business and their relationships with many of the employees brought unique perspectives to the board.

The children were instructed in how a board should conduct its meetings and how to construct and follow an agenda. They were taught the importance of the financial statements, how to read and interpret them, and the importance of giving their opinion and listening to the opinions of others without past, childish, family-influenced judgements.

Joanna, Vernon and Anthony proved to be vital members of the board. They quickly learned how to read the financial statements and gave great input and well thought-out opinions concerning the overall operations of the company.

All three went on to college; Joanna and Vernon graduated and took jobs outside the company. Joanna became an executive with an automotive distributor and Vernon with a financial institution. Anthony decided to study in the medical field. They all remained on the board of advisors and continued to contribute to the success of the company.

As Stan and Nena began to work on succession planning and financial security issues with their advisors, one of the options discussed was the possibility of the children coming into the business. Another option was to sell the business; a third was to hire a general manager to handle the day to day operations. This person could serve as a coach to any of the next generation who wanted to enter the family business.

Each of the Burgs children expressed a desire to keep the business within the family. As a result, Joanna entered the business full-time, as another division was established. The expertise she had gained at the automotive distributor, as well as her previous experience in the family business, proved invaluable to this start up division. Vernon also decided to enter the business. Because of his experience outside and his history within, Vernon also fit in well with the company structure.

But before Joanna and Vernon entered the business, an individual was hired who could take over day to day operations to enable Stan to focus on the numbers and develop plans to expand the company. An Operations Manager, Jerod, was chosen from a strong list of candidates. He was in line with the vision and culture of the family and business and became a very good fit. He helped grow the business, expand the teams in the field, and take over the operational side of the business.

After a few years, and after Joanna and Vernon had returned to the business, a president, Luke, was hired and Stan became CEO. This enabled Stan to concentrate on a company strategic plan and possible expansion and gave him time to become a mentor to the company leaders, especially Joanna and Vernon as well as the new President. Luke handled the day to day operations of the entire company and also took on the role of coach to the company managers.

Due to their ability to keep the communication lines open between the family and the company leaders, the Burgs' business continues to grow sales and profits above the normal.

Yes, the Burgs are extraordinary. The way they support one another, the respect they have for one another's opinions and how they come together to make decisions places them above a "normal dysfunctional" family business.

What is on the horizon for them? They are in the midst of finalizing a trust that will protect each family member as well as family investments. They have restructured the corporation to be in line with the structure of the trust.

Joanna has married and continues to work within the business. Both she and Vernon have increased their knowledge of the industry and have gained the respect of the employees. They are no longer viewed as being in their positions just because they are members of the family.

The management team is being restructured again as the success of the business makes it necessary to have people positioned for growth. The board of advisor's meetings are structured, with an agenda that allows room for innovative thinking and brainstorming.

The family supports one another in trying new things, and the parents continue to encourage their children to follow their dreams no matter what they are. With that in mind, Vernon has made it known that he would like to try his hand at a music career. All the advisory board members are supportive of him in this decision. Discussion was held on how he would still be able to contribute to the company as well as follow his dream.

As a family, the Burgs are making plans that support Vernon with the best interest of the family and the business in mind. Love of the family, support and understanding of individual dreams, combined with a true concern over the success of the family and the business, are the driving forces behind their decisions.

Key people are being groomed in a number of positions and Stan has seriously taken on the role of mentor and Servant Leader.

Stan and Nena are able to trust that the company is in good hands when they decide to take a much needed rest. Although, as a true entrepreneur, Stan still keeps an eye on the business, even when on vacation. That is the only dysfunction he needs to be cured of—although most entrepreneurs wouldn't call that a dysfunction.

> The business continues to grow in sales and profitability. The Burgs make plans and budgets for each year and are continually looking for innovative ways to grow the business.
>
> What will be happening in five years or 10 years from now? No one knows for sure, with the exception that there will be changes in the company. One certainty is that whatever the changes, whatever the decisions, the Burg family will make it together with prayerful thought and due diligence. And that is extraordinary!

Trust When Given First Is Returned

Do you trust your family? Do you trust that your family will always support you to others?

In a family business, all the members must be honest with one another while they support one another at work and in public. The family must consistently give the example of a unified front. They must demonstrate loyalty to one another that does not show any cracks or disruptions. All disagreements must be behind closed doors, away from outside ears and kept in the family.

No one wants to work for, or do business with, families who openly fight, who talk negatively about one another, who don't trust one another, and who rarely show support for one another. Employees and customers begin to think, "They don't even trust one another, why would they trust me or support me? Or give me the best deal?" When this happens customer count goes down and hiring good people becomes more difficult.

Jealousy, over-inflated egos, immature interaction as well as a win/lose mentality over decisions, have no place in a family business. Spouses must show support for one another, siblings must treat one another as equals, children and parents must respect one another and communicate openly with one another.

Families in business who trust one another make better, quicker decisions and are trusted more by employees and customers. They also are overall more successful than families in business who don't trust one another. Without trust family relationships deteriorate and the business suffers.

How does your family in business stack up? If your family does not have the trust of, and for, one another isn't it time you did something about it?

More Thoughts on Trust

Trust begins with the assumption that the people you deal with will be trustworthy. Your honest evaluations of each other determine how well you show trust to others.

Do you keep your word? Do you show respect to others for what they think and for them as equals? Are you reliable and honest? Do people have confidence in you? Do they really believe that you will not take advantage of them or harm them in any way?

KWAISERISM

Complete trust in one another is a basis for the transformation of a dysfunctional family business into an extraordinary family business.

Mistrust can become a habit, causing you to not trust others and others to not trust you. To get trust from others you have to be trustworthy. When you are trustworthy, most people will earn your trust as well. Your trustworthy employees will help you get rid of the ones who are not; people generally like living and working in a mutual trustworthy environment. Does your business and home have that type of environment?

FINAL COMMENTS FROM JIM

Our family is normal—We are dysfunctional!

We have presented our C.H.A.L.L.E.N.G.E.S. process (Chapters 2 – 11) that positively impacts the success of families in business. When properly addressed they will be the catalyst to transforming the family and business from the dysfunctional to the extraordinary. None of these C.H.A.L.L.E.N.G.E.S. are difficult to accomplish, yet the failure of families to commit to each has led to the breakdown of family relationships and business failure.

Each of the C.H.A.L.L.E.N.G.E.S. must be addressed by the family members until a consensus is reached and an agreement made on how the family is going to resolve each. A consensus that is good for the individual, the couple, the family, and the business must go hand in hand with the understanding that each of the C.H.A.L.L.E.N.G.E.S. is essential in the success of the family and the business. The many stories shared in this book give validity to that claim.

Because the rate of failure of family businesses is so high, and communication issues are at the start of each of the C.H.A.L.L.E.N.G.E.S., we knew that the commitment to change how families interact with one another would be a key driver of our consultations. There would have to be a commitment to move away from confrontation and family competition to loving, caring, and a focus on mutual success. Our experiences have enabled us to be convinced that with this commitment the family would overcome all adversity that will come their way.

Change can be scary. Most people don't want to consciously go through it. Most don't really ask for it, just like no one asked to be born. We enter the world not knowing where we are going or how to get there. We grow up with the challenges of trying to make friends, accomplish something that will get us noticed, or keep us from being noticed, compete with others for a job, find a partner, raise a family. We unconsciously go through change and only fear it when we begin to think about it.

Most entrepreneurs are not like other people in their feelings about change. Change comes when they find that they can't, or don't want to, work for anyone else. It comes when they start their own businesses to provide for their families. Rarely do entrepreneurs start a business thinking, "This will be my *family's* business!"

Then, one day, without fully realizing how this happened, our spouses, our children, their spouses and other family members are working in the business. A whole new set of changes, of challenges, appears. Sibling rivalry, individual emotion, poor communication in hope of avoiding conflict, and accusations of favoritism take over and the real challenges begin.

KWAISERISM

As you travel the road of life, enjoy every day. Enjoy your family, let go of envy and competition. For the journey will be over before you know it, and you will miss those who travelled with you, especially family.

Without the commitment of the family to treat one another differently, to change from competing with and treating one another as "little kids," to treating one another as equal adults, the emotions of each individual will always create dysfunction. Whether deciding on the direction of the company, who is in charge of what area, who makes what decisions and how will succession take place, the family business, without that commitment to one another, is filled with emotion. Parents, children, siblings, in-laws, spouses and other family members all contribute to the emotions a family in business must face.

The majority of our clients come to us with succession planning in mind. Only a very few are actually ready to deal with the issues of succession.

As you have read in previous chapters, poor communication (including the unspeakables) and inter-family conflict, both which are part of the failure to address the emotional issues, along with lack of FAMILY FIRST commitment are at the center of most family business challenges. Each of those issue areas also lead to organizational and operational issues that must be resolved before succession planning, before any planning can successfully take place. Not addressing and resolving them leads to the destruction of family relationships and to failed businesses.

But it does not have to be that way! Placing the success of the FAMILY FIRST is not just the right thing to do, it is smart business. When families are committed to the success of one another they all become successful. They are better able to make the necessary changes without any feeling of rivalry or mistrust. Only then can succession successfully be addressed.

Our hope is that you and your family will find the courage, out of love and respect for one another, to make the commitment to address and resolve your C.H.A.L.L.E.N.G.E.S.

We pray you and your family will use the proven principles and processes in this book and truly transform your business from the "dysfunctional" to the "extraordinary."

RECOMMENDED PUBLICATIONS AND **REFERENCES**

Ann Marie and I have read a substantial number of books on behavior, leadership, family businesses, general business, etc., both new ones and old ones. The books in this list are those we are so familiar with their words have become second nature to us.

These books are the ones we recommend you read before all others. Pick and choose what works for you out of each, and use these bits of wisdom to help your family and business.

We learn from many sources and each becomes a part of our lives. We hope you will use and pass on some of our thoughts and "Kwaiserisms" to others.

God Bless you, your family and your business!

GOOD BOOKS WE RECOMMEND AND SOME WE USED AS REFERENCE MATERIALS FOR THIS BOOK

God. The *Bible*. Kennedy and Sons Publishing, 1970.

Blanchard, Ken, and Johnson, Spencer. *One Minute Manager.* Harper, 1982.

Bolton, Robert. *People Skills.* Simon and Schuster, 1979.

Briner, Bob, and Pritchard, Ray. *The Leadership Lessons of Jesus.* Briner Pritchard, 1997.

Collins, Jim. *Good to Great.* Harper, 2001.

Collins, James, and Porras, Jerry. *Built to Last.* Harper Business, 1994.

Columbus, Craig, and Hendrickson, Mark. *God and Man on Wall Street.* Brick Tower Press, 2012.

Corbett, David. *The Portfolio Life.* Jossey Bass, 2007.

Covey, Steven. *The Seven Habits of Highly Successful People.* Simon and Schuster, 1989.

Goldratt, Eliyahu. *Critical Chain.* River Press, 1997.

Goldratt, Eliyahu. *The Goal.* River Press, 1992.

Greenleaf, Robert. *Servant Leadership.* Paulist Press, 1991.

Horasger, David. *The Trust Edge.* Free Press/Simon and Schuster, 2009.

Kennedy, Eugene. *Crisis Counseling.* Continuum, 1986.

Kidder, Rushworth. *Moral Courage.* Harper, 2006.

Kwaiser, Jim, Covey, Steven, and Blanchard, Ken. *The Roadmap to Success.* Insight Publishing, 2009.

Mandino, Og. *The Greatest Salesman in the World.* Fell, 2001.

Peters, Thomas, and Waterman, Robert. *In Search of Excellence.* Harper, 1982.

Robinson and Robinson. *Performance Counseling.* Barrett-Koehler, 1995.

Sujansky, Joanne, and Ferri-Reed, Jan. *Keeping the Millennials.* Wiley, 2009.

Tobe, Jeff. *Coloring Outside the Lines.* The Business Conference Press, 2001.

Tobe, Jeff, and Thomas, Bill. *Anticipate: Knowing what Customers Need Before They Do.* John Wiley & Sons, 2013.

Warren, Arnie. *The Great Connection.* Pullman Books, 1997.

Warren, Rick. *The Purpose-Driven Life.* Zondervan, 2002.

SOME ADDITIONAL RESOURCES AND RECOMMENDED READINGS

American Management Services, Inc. newsletters, www.amserv.com.

Business Newsletter, http://terrypbrock.com/newsletter.

Campden Family Business Magazine, www.camdenfb.com.

Creativity Blog, www.jefftobe.com/blog.

Family Business Magazine, www.familybusinessmagazine.com.

The Futurist Newsletter, https://futureinsightnesletter.com.

Kennesaw State University Coles College of Business, Family Business Global Survey, www.elance.com/q/global-businesssurvey.com.

KPMG's Family Business Survey, www.KPMG.com.

Kreischer Miller's Family Business Survey, www.KMCO.com/wp/wp-content/uploads/2016-kreischer-miller

Private Wealth Magazine, www.fa-mag.com/private-wealth.

ROCG America's Business Succession Survey, www.ROCG.com.

U.S. Department of Labor Bureau of Labor Statistics, www.bis.gov.

www.challengesinc.com

www.kabusinessplanners.com

jim@challengesinc.com

ann@challengesinc.com

Which of the C.H.A.L.L.E.N.G.E.S. should be the top priorities for your family?

What are you going to do to address these priorities and transform your family business from dysfunctional to extraordinary?